D1527172

Nepali Visions, Nepali Dreams

The Poetry of Laxmiprasad Devkota

Modern Asian Literature Series

Nepali Visions, Nepali Dreams

The Poetry of Laxmiprasad Devkota

with translations of selected poems

by David Rubin

Columbia University Press

New York 1980

The author and publisher gratefully acknowledge the generous support given them by the National Endowment for the Humanities. Research leading to this book was funded in part by a Fellowship for Independent Study and Research, and publication has been assisted by a further grant from the Endowment.

UNESCO COLLECTION OF REPRESENTATIVE WORKS
NEPALESE SERIES
This book
has been accepted
in the Nepalese Series
of the Translations Collection
of the United Nations
Educational, Scientific and Cultural Organization
(UNESCO)

Columbia University Press
New York   Guildford, Surrey

Library of Congress Cataloging in Publication Data
Devkota, Laxmi Prasad, 1908–1959.
Nepali visions, Nepali dreams.
(Modern Asian literature series)
Bibliography: p.
I. Rubin, David George.
PK2598.D37A27   891'.49   80-106
ISBN 0-231-05014-3

To the Poets of Nepal

Modern Asian Literature Series

Editorial Board

❧Contents

❧Preface

The comparatively young literature of Nepal swiftly reached its first full maturity with the work of Laxmiprasad Devkota (1909–1959). He is one of many fine Nepali poets of this century, but he is clearly the most remarkable in terms of originality, depth, and the variety and resourcefulness of his poetic techniques. He is particularly distinguished by his success in infusing his work with a genuine Nepali character and color. This is not merely a matter of treating Nepali subject matter—for many others have done that—or of a superficial identification with local traditions and national aspirations. Rather (and one thinks of Yeats or Frost or Nirala) Devkota achieves an extraordinary fusion of popular diction with a unique personal utterance. This is all the more remarkable in the case of a poet who was notorious for his speed and carelessness in composition and who failed to edit or even correct any but a handful of poems in his immense *oeuvre*.

It is perhaps too early to attempt a definitive study of Devkota's work. As of this writing some twenty to twenty-five volumes of his writing are yet to be published, while more poems and essays continue to come to light. There is no collected edition of his work, and several volumes are at present out of print. Existing printings show a wide variance, and manuscripts, in the opinion of many Nepali critics and editors, are full of indecipherable passages.

My intention in undertaking this book has been first of all to present in English translation a selection of some of Devkota's poems in the hope of suggesting their quality, charm, and variety, and then to describe in some detail Devkota's life and work. It is my belief that his finest poetry is found in the long poems (*mahākāvya*, epics), such as *Sulocanā*, the *Nepālī*

Śākuntala, and *Prometheus,* but it has seemed wiser to represent him by complete poems—mostly short lyrics—rather than by fragments of the long narratives. Some passages from these narratives will be found in the Introduction, as well as one short excerpt from *Circe the Enchantress* among the translations.

As Devkota is also one of the most interesting and stylistically vigorous of Nepali prose writers, I have made a point of translating fairly extensive passages from his *Essays* and other critical writings in the Introduction.

This book, then, is clearly only a beginning, one that I hope may provide an impetus for the further study not only of Devkota but of all the literature of modern Nepal, still virtually unknown outside its homeland. It is a literature immensely rich in itself and indispensable for the insight it offers into the indigenous culture of the Himalayan kingdoms.

⚜Acknowledgments

I would like to express my gratitude to Mrs. Laxmiprasad Devkota and to Mr. Padma Prasad Devkota for their consent to the publication of my translations of Mahakavi Devkota's poetry and their help in making available to me unpublished works of the poet and the interviews tape-recorded at Shanta Bhavan in September 1959; to Mr. Devkota, Mahes Raj Pant of the Nepal Research Centre, and Professor Dor Bahadur Bista of Tribhuvan University for their patient help in clarifying many difficult passages in the poet's work; to Miss Rita Goldman, International Communication Agency, Rangoon, for first putting me in touch with the Devkota family and transcribing on cassette the tape-recorded interviews; to Karen Mitchell of Columbia University Press and Neil Gross for their painstaking reading of the manuscript of this book and many valuable suggestions; to Mr. Gross and Professor Barbara Stoler Miller of Barnard College for their help with Sanskrit metrical questions; and to Professor Theodore Riccardi, Jr., of Columbia University for first bringing Devkota to my attention and for his subsequent encouragement with this project. I would also like to express my deep appreciation to the United States Educational Foundation in Nepal and the National Endowment for the Humanities for their generous support during the time I have worked on this book.

The poems "Clay Lamp," "I Said" (1 and 2), "He Said," "A Thousand Deaths A Thousand Lives," and "Crazy" have appeared in *Translation*.

◄§A Note on Transliteration

In the following pages diacritical marks, with few exceptions, are given only for titles of works and passages quoted from the original Nepali. In such instances, the transliteration of Nepali, Sanskrit, or Hindi names or words follows the system adopted by the International Congress of Orientalists at Athens in 1912, with some exceptions in the matter of nasalization, described below. The final short "a," inherent in terminal consonants or at the end of certain syllables, which is almost always silent in modern Hindi and only occasionally sounded in Nepali, is omitted in transliterating words from these languages except when following a conjunct consonant (i.e., *kāvya* or *yuddha*) or when actually pronounced, as in Nepali *"bihāna"* or *"garera."* In the case of titles which are actually Sanskrit compounds (*Rāvaṇ-Jaṭāyu-Yuddha*) I have transliterated according to Nepali pronunciation (hence no "a" at the end of *Rāvaṇ*). In the case of *Nepālī Śākuntala* I have regarded *"Śākuntala"* as a Sanskrit word, since it has no independent existence as a Nepali word, and should not be confused with the heroine's Sanskrit name, *Śakuntalā*.

For the most part, the various types of nasalization are indicated simply by "n," as the Devanagari spellings in Nepali are extremely inconsistent, words containing such nasals sometimes being spelled two and even three different ways on a single page.

As the name of the poet is consistently translated "Laxmi" in Nepal, I have followed this style except in Nepali titles and quotations. Wherever there are fairly standardized English forms for Sanskrit terms or names (e.g., Sankhya, Shiva, Shakuntala, Dushyanta, or Lakshmi, when this refers to the goddess), these will be used except in titles or quotations.

xiii

Laxmiprasad Devkota: His Life and Work and His Place in Nepali Literature

Nepali Language and Literature Before Devkota

The Nepali language is a member of the Indo-European family, classified as a branch of the North Indian group, related to Western Hindi, Gujerati, and Panjabi, among others. Like Bengali, Nepali has lost gender except (to a limited extent) in personal pronouns and certain verb forms referring specifically to women. Noun inflection has virtually disappeared, and plurals are indicated by a suffix, if at all. Nepali shares with Hindi a characteristic wealth of subtle and expressive verbal compounds, but it possesses a much greater variety of tense forms, many of them exact parallels with no real distinction in meaning. There are, for instance, three forms of the conjunctive particle, each with a different number of syllables (e.g., *garī, garera,* and *garīkana,* all present participles of *garnu,* to do), potentially most useful to poets in working out metrical problems. The language is also rich in expressions known as *anukaraṇ,* onomatopoeic or otherwise suggestive words, often rhyming, such as *ukus-mukus* to express the uncomfortable feeling of congestion, either atmospheric or digestive, or *ṭuplukka* for "suddenly, in the nick of time." Nepali poets use these expressions freely, and none has exploited them more than Laxmiprasad Devkota. Another peculiarity of the language is the large number of particles, mostly monosyllabic, used to modify the tone of a statement, conveying surprise, emphasis, deprecation, affection, and the like. Both a skillful poet and a resourceful conversationalist may use these with great subtlety to convey complexity of tone.

Nepali is still evolving more rapidly than most European languages, and there is considerable disagreement as to what constitutes a proper standard. This fact may contribute to the adventurousness and whimsicality of some modern poets, most particularly Devkota, in matters of diction and syntax.

Although the earliest inscriptions in Nepali go back to the fourteenth century and serious literature in that language has been produced from the time Prithvi Narayan Shah completed the occupation of the Kathmandu Valley towns in the eighteenth century, almost all the important writing of Nepal dates from after the First World War.[1]

The credit for giving Nepali its first important work goes to Bhanu Bhakta (1814–1868), who wrote a version of the *Rāmāyaṇa* (based largely on the medieval Sanskrit *Adhyāt-marāmāyaṇa* and drawing as well from Tulsi's late-sixteenth-century Avadhi *Rāmcaritmānas*), a poem which gained universal popularity throughout Nepal and gave a tremendous boost to the language as a serious literary medium.[2]

Before Devkota the most important names in twentieth-century Nepali literature are Lekhnath Paudyal (1884–1965) and Balkrishna Sama (1903–).[3] Lekhnath, in his lyrics and the narrative poem *Taruṇ-Tapasi* (The Young Ascetic), brought a new refinement and grace of expression to the language; for this reason Nepali critics count his work as the beginning of the modern era. Balkrishna Sama has achieved fame both as dramatist and narrative poet. His work is considered more intellectual than emotional, and its passion tends toward the polemical.

In Laxmiprasad Devkota modern Nepali poetry reaches full maturity with a kind of explosion. Devkota wrote prodigiously in all forms, and today, two decades after his death, there are more than twenty of his books still to be published. He was a poet "of the flood," in his own expression, "not a light shower." He rarely took time to rewrite his work or even edit it, with the result that it is of uneven quality, occasionally repetitious, and frequently suffers from obscurities, some of which may simply be lapses of the pen. What is remarkable is that Devkota's muse so rarely flags in such a vast *oeuvre*.

4

Among his best works the long narrative *Nepālī Śakuntala* (443 pages) was written in three months, and the almost equally long *Sulocanā* in ten days. During the fifty years of his life he also found time to do translations, teach, fill a post as cabinet minister, and travel extensively, mostly in India, to represent Nepal at literary conferences. The evolution in his poetry is not easy to trace because of the difficulty in dating many of his works, but it is clear that he experimented ceaselessly and aimed generally for greater simplicity and directness in his later work. In an essay written in 1957,[4] he himself cites obscurity and over-sanskritization, along with too great a readiness to coin new words, as his major faults. In a way, Devkota may be said to constitute an entire literature in himself. He dwarfs his contemporaries, from whom he is always unmistakably distinct, while writers of the post-Devkota era demonstrate a very different spirit—ironic, naturalistic, or cerebral. In Devkota we see the entire Romantic era of Nepali literature.

Laxmiprasad Devkota:
The Poet's Life

According to tradition, the Devkotas, a family of Purbiya Brahmans, came from somewhere in Kanauj, in India, the same region that had been the ancestral homeland of the Hindi poets Nirala and Pant, though both were born outside Kanauj. After living in various parts of Nepal, chiefly in Jumla district in the far west of the country, the Devkotas settled finally in Kathmandu soon after Prithvi Narayan Shah had made it the capital of his new kingdom in 1768. From the beginning of their time in the Valley the Devkotas were active as writers, poets, and teachers. The family made their home first in Bhotahity; Til Madhav, the future poet's father, moved to Kamal Pokhri Thatunati, close to Dilli Bazar, and here the poet was born on November 12, 1909 (1966 v.s. Kartik 27 *gate*, according to the Nepali calendar), the third son of Til Madhav's second wife. Since the day that year coincided with Tihar, the festival consecrated to Lakshmi, the child was named in her honor. Lakshmi, the goddess of wealth and prosperity, is traditionally at odds with Sarasvati, the goddess of the arts and learning. Lakshmi's hostility to the artist was to prove no exception in the case of this child of Sarasvati despite the tribute of his naming. The family was to be a large one, with two daughters from the first wife surviving into adulthood and six boys and seven girls born to Àmar Rajyalaxmi, the second wife.

At home Devkota began the formal study of Nepali, Sanskrit, and a little English. Til Madhav Devkota was the author of several poems in Sanskrit, odes and hymns for the most part, along with some poetry in Nepali. Laxmiprasad would often copy down his father's works, learning them by heart as he did so, and it is no doubt the influence of his elderly father (67 at the time) that accounts for the tone of the poet's first known poem, written in 1919 when he was ten:

> Know the world to be a sea of deep sorrow, brother;
> be not proud—we must go.[5]

Although his father wished him to be a pandit, a Brahman learned in the texts and necessarily expert in Sanskrit, the rest of the family, feeling that the boy could learn enough Sanskrit at home, wanted him to enroll in the Darbar High School, where he could become proficient in English. Devkota began to attend that school in 1921, and there, a couple of years later, he made his first attempts at poetry in English.

His preoccupation with financial problems had begun long before. He recalled in an essay that when he was eight his brother Lekhnath, having passed his matriculation examinations from Calcutta, was earning two to three hundred rupees a month from teaching; this vocation became Laxmiprasad's ideal. "I must earn, I must learn English, I must become a Master!"[6] This ambition was constantly encouraged by the rest of the family.

In the spring of 1925, at fifteen, he was married to Mandevi, a Kathmandu girl of a Chalise Brahman family. In 1926 he took the matriculation examination from Patna University and passed with a first class, and the following year he enrolled in Trichandra College to study science. He describes himself in these days as being under the spell of Wordsworth. He had become unpopular with the family because he "wouldn't make the slightest effort to run their errands or do their shopping for them."[7] He had also become, he said, a "dreadful snob about English being the salvation of the country." At about this time he began his teaching, some ten to twelve hours a day. In 1928 his first child, Savitri, was born. More and more interested in literature, he gave up his plan for a degree in science and opted for a B.A. degree, which he received in 1930 from Patna for work in English, mathematics, and economics. His was the only B.A. awarded in all of Nepal that year.

At this time he was still committed to English as his literary language.

> . . . I did not speak Nepali, I would not speak it with people who spoke Nepali. But I would pour out English to anyone I met in the street who spoke it. It seemed to me as though there were no words in Nepali, that feelings could not be expressed, as though Nepali were not a language of scholars. If I did speak Nepali, my tongue—which I'd been polishing with thirteen years of education—got all mixed up. I used to think in English, speak only in English. . . . If I spoke Nepali the students became insolent, if I spoke English I humiliated them. . . . The pandits I saw as fossils, superannuated, unaware of the light of modernism; bigoted, narrow, and without learning, pouring out all that medieval Indian deep sleep over their heads.[8]

Also in 1930 Devkota was arrested, along with several other young intellectuals, for signing a proposal for opening a public library. The sentence for this was three years rigorous imprisonment, which was suspended on payment of 100 rupees and the signing of a document stipulating that the defendants would not again engage in activities for the public welfare on pain of twelve years rigorous imprisonment. This was the beginning of Devkota's long battle with the repressive Rana regime, which would terminate only with the revolution of 1950–1951.[9]

In 1931 Devkota went to Patna in India to study for his bachelor of law degree.[10] The following year Prakash, the first of his sons, was born. In 1934 he received his LL.B. (second division) and would have gone for his Master of Law had not family economic problems obliged him to return to Kathmandu. At this time he refused an offer of a government post, preferring to teach.

In 1934 his mother died, and the following year his father as well. Between these two events his first poem to be published appeared in a winter issue of the daily *Gorkhāpatra* (Marg 15 *gate* 1991), with the title "Ocean of the Full Moon."

From this time on poems began to appear regularly, many of them somewhat sentimentalized genre poems ("The Poor Man," 1934; "The Peasant," 1936; "The Gardener," 1940), with the influence of Wordsworth very apparent in the emphasis on the fundamental goodness of humble people, the importance of nature, and fondness for recollection and childhood ("Childhood," 1938). There are Nepalized versions of "Lucy Gray" ("Cāru," 1940) and "The Solitary Reaper" ("Her Reaping Song," 1935) and an ode called "Memory" (1935).[11] Some of the poems, notably "The Beggar" (1940) and "Pilgrim" (1941), show tendencies toward a harsher realism and satire of religious orthodoxy. This is also the period that saw the creation of the first of Devkota's many long narrative poems and still his most popular work, *Munā Madan* (Muna and Madan), published in March–April 1936. Written in a popular folk meter called *jhyāure*, the poem is daring for its time. The story, which bears some similarity to Tennyson's *Enoch Arden*, is also his first treatment of *viraha* or *viyoga*, the separation of lovers—an important theme in Sanskrit epic and *kāvya* literature and one that was to be the great theme of most of Devkota's mature work as represented in the narrative poems.

In an essay of this period, "The Fifteenth of Asarh," which was his first published prose, the poet describes a harvest festival in idyllic English Romantic terms, celebrating above all the peasant's spontaneous sense of rhythm and poetic diction. As a sample he cites a folksong (which sounds suspiciously like one of his own compositions):

> Harvest time—lightning flashes—showers sing a song;
> the river leaps beneath the clouds, making my heart dance.
> Today my blouse is decorated with the fancy embroidery of
>   the mud.
> Laughter today and singing today—
> Alas for tomorrow! who weeps if death harvests him?[12]

Earlier he had drawn a contrast between the peasants and the poets of Kathmandu, such as those, like himself, who were published in literary magazines like *Śāradā* (which incidentally also published the essay):

Here there was singing, poetry; the extempore poets could move their pens as quickly as Sarasvati her tongue. On one side questions, from the other immediate answers, and in rhythmic, melodious meters. It seemed as though the poems in *Śāradā* were only laborious metrical exercises. Here there was an unbroken flow, a welling up, such as cannot be found in all the congealed fragments in that journal. After hearing the voices of these people it seemed as though embellishment, rhyme, and metaphor were burdens, impediments to poetry. In them was the simple sweetness which is only in the language of emotion but is not found in the language of thought. When an intense feeling touches even the most ordinary man, then in his utterance there appears an extraordinary esthetic quality [*ras*]. . . . They do not *make;* they draw it out from within. In us is the cleverness of words, in them the sweetness of emotion.[13]

In all his subsequent esthetic formulations Devkota was to characterize his own work as having flow *(pravāh)* and emotion *(bhāv)*, in opposition to thought *(vicār)*.

In January 1939 Devkota went to the sanitarium at Ranchi,

9

in India, for four months to recover from a severe mental depression. He refers to this event in the poem "Crazy" ("Pāgal") of 1953, and describes the circumstances as follows:

> . . . You know that I was in financial trouble at that time. Everywhere the awareness of my insignificance struck me. I considered myself the smallest creature in the world. I saw others as mountains. For financial reasons I found it impossible to satisfy any of my wishes. Nobody understood my mental anguish at this time. I would sit for the whole day engaged in such thoughts. Because of this, the idiots, not understanding what was wrong, thinking me crazy, hauled me off to Ranchi. But I was suffering from economic disease. What could a doctor do? Nevertheless, I remained in Dr. Berkeley Hill's care for a few months to satisfy them. He understood my illness and said, "It's a geographical mistake! You should have been born in the West and you were born in the East." Perhaps his meaning was, If you were in the West you wouldn't be suffering financial distress while in the East you're afflicted with economic burdens. Though he tried, my "congenital illness" did not improve.[14]

A perusal of the correspondence among Devkota's brothers concerning the illness does not shed much light on what was wrong. Devkota is chided for smoking too much, nervousness, unwarranted melancholy. Dr. Berkeley Hill's recommendation was that when he left Ranchi Devkota should live outside Kathmandu, if possible, but certainly in a house away from his family.[15] "Family" here apparently signified that he should live apart from his brothers, not from his wife and children. Whatever the true nature of Devkota's mental state in 1938–1939, there is no other indication throughout his life of any psychological instability.

In 1938 he had gone with one of his brothers on a trip to Gosainthan, a mountain lake and pilgrimage site north of Kathmandu. The essay describing this trek ("Mountain Life") reveals an increasing sophistication in his point of view and a decline in the Wordsworthian idealism. The life of the peasants is difficult, beset with illness and crippled by illiteracy. The poet feels the immense temptation to devote himself, like some Indian writers, to their uplift and education, but he concludes, "my soul was much smaller than Premchand's; I was a victim of habit, a slave of custom." [16]

A new concern with Hindu orthodoxy is evident in Devkota's first short story, "Her Little Goat," published in *Śāradā* in 1939, dealing with a child's horror at the sacrifice of her pet goat for the Dasain festival. In this same year Devkota published a volume of Nepali translations of well-known essays of Bacon, Swift, Coleridge, and others.

At the beginning of 1941 Devkota took up residence in a section of Kathmandu called Maiti Devi in a house he named Kavi Kunj, "the poet's bower," where he was to reside until his death except for the two years of exile in Banaras. In 1943 he began to receive a very small monthly salary of 70 rupees from the Nepali Translation Association (Nepālī Bhāṣānuvād Pariṣad).

The forties were the most productive years of Devkota's career. In 1945 the long narrative poems *Nepālī Śakuntala* and *Kunjinī* and the collection of original essays appeared, followed by *Sulocanā* in 1946. Many other works not to be published for a decade or more—*Mahārāṇā Pratāp, Circe the Enchantress, Mhendu,* and the play *The Peasant Girl,* to cite a few—were written in this period.

In 1946 Devkota took up a post as professor of English at Trichandra College at an annual salary of 1200 rupees, and the next year he chaired the first meeting of the Nepali Literary Board (Nepālī Sāhitya Pariṣad). His speech brought his first recognition from Lekhnath Paudyal, the unofficial national laureate, who until that time had not regarded his work as of any significance.

Only a few days later Devkota, feeling suffocated by the Rana regime and the prevailing censorship, left for voluntary exile in Banaras. Two months later, while his house in Maiti Devi was under police watch, Krishna Prasad, his second son, died of typhoid at the age of eleven.

In Banaras Devkota took part in the meetings of the exiled Nepali Congress Party and edited *Yug Bānī,* a revolutionary journal. The works he wrote during his exile were of all kinds, including many revolutionary in tone. Of these the following is typical:

> We are not sleeping, we shall all rise
> in the name of God
> abandoning house food and clothing
> in the name of justice—
> if we give up our breath, our life,
> it's no great matter.
> We do not give up the justice man needs—
> we must surely die one day.
> Let us not live like beasts—
> if we are men let us live like men,
> let us bring man's justice.[17]

Devkota's productivity, always remarkable, was particularly unusual during this period, which saw the creation of—among so many other works—52 sonnets in English on the occasion of the death of Mahatma Gandhi. Much of this production, including many of the revolutionary poems, though their sincerity is undeniable, is inevitably hack work. As Devkota explains it:

At that time I was badly in need of money. I needed a publisher who would pay me for my poems and publish them. I found such a person in Tikadatt Djital, head of the Nepali Saubhagya Pustakalaya in Dudh-Vinayak. He agreed to take my poems for two rupees each. For a few days I gave him five poems each day. When my expenses rose I began to give him ten. He cut the fee for each poem in half. I gave him twenty-five poems. In a few days he halved his fee once more. By this progression the price of my poems fell to four annas. Nevertheless, I continued to give him poems to meet daily expenses. Finally he said, "Your poems have bankrupted me! I can't pay for any more." And I was in despair.[18]

In 1948 first his eldest son, Prakash, and then Mrs. Devkota joined the poet in Banaras. In 1949, after an attack of malaria, Devkota was persuaded by his wife to return to Kathmandu and the house in Maiti Devi. He was now completely out of funds, without any teaching post for income, and all in all in even more precarious economic straits than he had known in Banaras.

The final ten years of Devkota's life present a drama of unending financial distress and deteriorating health. While he tried to make a living out of various short-term appointments at Padma-Kanya College and the Commerce College, he was obliged to go into debt to defray medical expenses and dowries for his daughters' weddings. The somberness of these years was increased by the death of Prakash in 1952 at the age of eighteen. Devkota is reported to have said, more than once, to his wife, "Tonight let's abandon the children to the care of society, and you and I renounce this world at bedtime and take potassium cyanide or morphine or something like that." [19] But—extraordinarily—all personal accounts of Devkota during these melancholy times attest to his gaiety, vivacity, and enormous energy. His output was only slightly diminished; the poems later published in *Chaharā* (Cascades) and the children's volume *Sunko Bihāna* (Golden Morning), along with many stray lyrics, belong to this period. Much of what was published during these years had been written earlier, like the children's poems of *Putalī* (Butterfly), written between 1943 and 1947 and published in 1952.

Devkota was also occupied with editorial tasks, including the responsibility for the short-lived but important journal *Indrenī* (The Rainbow), in the seven issues of which he published some of his own most important poems (e.g., "Crazy" and "Song of the Storm"), along with English translations of a few of them. He was active on various committees, including the one established by King Tribhuvan for the founding of a university in Nepal, and served for a few months in 1957 as Minister of Education. In this same year the Royal Nepal Academy was established, something the poet for many years had striven for. With his membership in the academy he was awarded a monthly stipend of 600 rupees. Also in 1957 his last child, a son, was born.

During the fifties Devkota made several trips abroad to writers' conferences, including one almost every year to India, one each to Bucharest, Moscow, and Peking, and again to the Soviet Union in 1958 to address the Afro-Asian Writers Conference in Tashkent, after which he went to Moscow, where he spent twenty-eight days in the hospital.

His health had been poor for several years. In 1958 he had gone to Calcutta for treatment of a peptic ulcer. The diagnosis was cancer so advanced that no attempt was made at remedial surgery. Incongruously, but characteristically, at about this time Devkota completed a volume of humorous verse, *Manoranjan* (Entertainments). It was also typical of Devkota that after this experience he would undertake the trip to Tashkent in a condition so weakened that he needed a blood transfusion on his arrival, immediately following which he delivered a speech that by all accounts was extraordinary no less for its energy and brilliance than for its length, and after which he gave an extensive press interview.

During his last few months he spent several weeks in Shanta Bhavan, the United Mission Hospital in Patan, near Kathmandu, where he was attended by Dr. Edgar Miller, described by the poet in a dedication as "my medical angel." [20]

A second trip to Calcutta for medical consultations in the summer of 1959 proved fruitless. By this time, along with his declining health, Devkota's financial situation had deteriorated even further; during the last months of his life his medical expenses were defrayed by contributions from the King and other members of the royal family, along with donations from colleagues at the academy and even his students. In a speech Devkota made the day before his last trip to Calcutta, he expressed his gratitude for these contributions but earnestly requested that they be halted immediately.

Dr. Miller says that Devkota, in the last month of his life (spent mostly at Shanta Bhavan), expressed a desire to become a Christian, a conversion that was not legally possible in Nepal and would have caused the mission doctors considerable difficulties and possibly even expulsion from the country. On September 6 in a tape-recorded conversation he told Dr. Miller, "Christianity is a great religion and I appreciate it"; and, in connection with the work of the mission doctors, "This translation of spiritual teaching into practice is the greatest thing that man can do." [21] But there is no indication in any of his statements or in his final poems that his interest in Christianity moved beyond sympathy and admiration. He told his fellow poet and friend Madhav Ghimire that he wished to have the usual Hindu rites when he died.[22] His final poems in Nepali and English speak of both God and Krishna, never of Christ. In an English poem written ten days before his death he says "you/Find that this world is all poison,/God is the only consolation, your last stay." In a Nepali poem of the same day he wrote, "I learned Krishna was the only one (but) I did not become his devotee, nor find wisdom or knowledge." To Dr. Bethel Fleming he remarked, while conceding that God "is all love," "I sometimes am afraid that God is tired of seeking me—I have not sought him." [23] And in another conversation with Ghimire he described the soul as immaterial, a spark of fire, not conscious of God, ignorant of the way, and torturing itself in hellfire; and his own work he called no more than the product of an "anxiety neurosis." [24]

The state of Devkota's mind seems to have moved through many extremes during his last months, from despair to hope to resignation. More than once he asked visitors to give him potassium cyanide to end his suffering. To his wife he said, "*Bajyai,* how much money do you have now?" "*Buva hazur,* one or two hundred," she answered; Nityaraj Pande suggests that she fabricated this amount, wishing to spare her husband any further distress. Devkota went on, "If I last another three or four days you won't be able to feed me; that much money is just enough to pay for my last rites—let it go at that" (*bhaigo*— i.e., don't waste the money on keeping me alive any longer).[25]

He had been sustained by volunteer blood donations from his students. He told Dr. Miller that he saw no point in this[26] and wrote on September 11 to the editor of *Hāl Khabar:*

> I must thank you for the sympathy which you have shown me from the beginning until the present. Now I consider it altogether too painful to protract my life some eight or ten days with human blood. Better use of the blood now being given to me would be to donate it to some other sick person who can be saved.
>
> Two courageous young men, my nephew Padmanath Devkota and Bholaman Singh, have kept me alive for the last couple of days until this moment by their donations of blood. May they be blessed with long life. Now I shall not accept human blood; I give my thanks to those who have wanted to donate it.[27]

Devkota's imminent death had become something of a public event—extraordinary for Nepal. When according to the tradition of Nepali Hindus he was taken to Pashupatinath, on the banks of the Basumati, to die, he was visited by many of the most important people of the country, including the poet-laureate, Lekhnath Paudyal, and members of the royal family.[28] It was an ordeal of publicity such as few Nepalis have had to suffer, attended by the pain and grotesque irony of being prematurely transported to Pashupatinath to die and thence back to Shanta Bhavan for a few days more before the final transfer. Throughout this time, as an eyewitness reports, Devkota was sardonic, sometimes bitter, usually pessimistic, but not in the least given to self-pity.[29]

On September 14 Devkota asked for Dr. Miller to come to Pashupatinath. The doctor and two colleagues, by special order of the Prime Minister, were admitted into the shrine, normally closed to non-Hindus. Devkota joined his hands in *namaste,* a faint smile on his lips and tears starting in his eyes, and asked the doctor to pray for him. When he left, Dr. Miller saw hundreds of students streaming down the road from the city to the river shrine. Classes had been dismissed so that they could come to hold vigil until the poet's death, which occurred a little after six that evening.

Ideas on Art and Life

The fundamental element of creation is love
and the fundamental action of love is to give happiness.[30]

A day or so before he died Devkota told the poet Dom Moraes, "They called me a Communist, because I went to Russia . . . I was only a poet. . . ."[31]

It is true that Devkota was no ideologue. In both the poetry and the essays the impulse is prevailingly emotional rather than intellectual, the constant assertion of convictions based on intuition and faith. All his life Devkota was under the spell of the English Romantic poets. He imitates Wordsworth in the early poems and refers to him in the essays more frequently than to any other writer. His revolutionary impulse, like the Romantic poets', sprang from a generous nature outraged by social injustice, not from abstract principle, and never atrophied in rigid dogma. Some maintain that he espoused the Sankhya philosophy;[32] others see him as a dialectical materialist,[33] or merely as a humanist of the vaguest sort.[34] In matters of religion he is no easier to pin down. Nevertheless, a perusal of the poems and essays will serve to show that there is a fairly constant set of ideas throughout Devkota's work and that the apparent contradictions and confusions, when they exist at all, are such as one would find in the work of any poet who had no intention of presenting a theoretically consistent view of the world.

The pessimism of Devkota's first poem was no doubt a

child's mannered imitation of his father. But it was prophetic of the future reality. Later Devkota was to write:

> So long as I went on dreaming, borne along by life, finding happiness in the magic spell of "I'll do" and "I'll fulfill," I had no knowledge at all of what renunciation meant, even though I had sometimes written poems about the world being a dream, insipid. One assumes the true form of renunciation only when it springs from an inner awareness, and the soul of renunciation comes into being only from the awareness of the worthlessness of worldly things, rising inward through the experience of the sorrow of sensual existence.[35]

The real experience of the tragedies arising from attachment to worldly objects was not long in coming. For Devkota the attachment was found most intensely in the form of love for his family and friends. With money—no matter how much he suffered from the lack of it—he had always been careless, like Nirala a legend for his prodigal generosity while in need himself. Though he was extremely fond of travel, good food, and gambling, he seems to have remained free of any ambition for life in the grand style. As for success, it came early enough so that he did not have to mope longing for renown. The real losses can be seen in the deaths of his parents, of two of his sons in childhood, and of a daughter two months after her birth, as well as in the years of exile from his beloved Nepal. All this no doubt contributed largely to the darkness of the world view expressed in many of the poems and to his predilection for the unhappy ending. The over-all theme of much of the poet's major work is *viraha* or *viyoga*, the separation of lover from beloved or creature from creator, the great underlying emotional basis for so much of Sanskrit and later Indian literature.[36] And although Devkota's interest in *viraha* must have arisen in part from its inherent potential for drama and pathos, as well as from something fundamental to his immersion in classical Indian culture, it seems clear that the poet had developed, from his personal experience of the world, a strong conviction of the profoundly tragic character of human life.

This is not to suggest that Devkota was a gloomy or saturnine man. He was, in fact, of a decidedly joyous temperament in his gregariousness, love of nature, and the sense of humor that is characteristic of so many of his poems. As with many other genuine pessimists, his world-sorrow came from a love of the world, not a hatred of it. His pessimism aligns him more with a late Victorian like Arnold than with the Romantics he so much admired. It is, I believe, precisely the contradiction between his exuberant idealism and his often somber naturalism that gives Devkota's work its distinctive tension.

Throughout the essays and poems nature is held up as the best teacher. "The cuckoo learns to sing without a teacher; the brook needs no instructor to move along in the path of its rhythm."[37]

> . . . I hold the opinion that Nature is superior to learning, and destiny to regulations. The human soul shows its direction by its natural inclination, and where the heart is most involved man finds his delight.[38]

Or again:

> That our books of learning and scriptures, imprisoned in hair-splitting distinctions, had finally rendered man useless I understood when, eyes failing, going blind in the atrocities of black print, [I realized] that man's soul had begun to wither from the absence of natural truth. Human philosophies play the whirlwind but the straight truth of nature shines fresh in the breeze.[39]

"When he sees a flower man is ashamed of his unbeautiful life."[40] "I began the study of the true when I left college and started to see life."[41]

In the passage from "The Fifteenth of Asarh" quoted in the last section (p. 9), we saw Devkota discovering true poetry not in the literary journals but in the songs of the peasant reapers. Again like Wordsworth, as well as Rousseau and so many other Romantic writers, he finds inspiration in the child, and this is reflected by the many poems he wrote for children,

19

including those collected in *Sunko Bihāna* (Golden Morning) and the two volumes of *Putalī* (Butterfly). Of his infant daughter he wrote, ". . . I became gradually awakened by her baby talk. . . . she began to make clear to me a father's heart, and it seemed to me as though there were a God."[42] The innocence of his childlike heroines, whether mythic or drawn from contemporary life—Muna (bud), Mhendu (flower), Sulocana and Shakuntala—is associated with their closeness to nature and their love of flowers, gardens, and trees. For the flower in its fragility "is a reprimand to all the selfishness and greed of my soul."[43]

Again like the British Romantics, he finds a value in the status of the humble. "There is a joy in being small; one is able to see the greatness of others dancing in the swords and plumes they wear. In passions at peace is bliss; one can watch the pomp of others."[44] So too the true gentleman is a natural man, whereas the *poseur*, sometimes mistaken for a gentleman, affects a stammer, makes a pretense of hemming and hawing.[45] True nobility is more likely to be found in the country. So he will write, after describing the hardships of mountain life, the poor nourishment, the stunted children:

> Here there is not the glitter of the city, nor the roar, which—with all the inner mechanism of mankind shuddering and groaning—disturbs the natural nobility of life; here there is none of the artificiality that wreaks such outrages on the human soul—life is natural here.[46]

And Nature is responsible above all for the inspiration of the artist.

> We often deride a novice poet with the epithet "a gurgling brook." But why will the beauty-worshipping imaginations of future poets continue to find their first inspiration in the gurgling sound of water? In it there must be some primordial essence. What do our awakened hearts discover in it? What influence? We may investigate the basic elements of beauty where the natural inclination of youth grows impatient to seek out the ingredients of bliss.[47]

From this point it is not surprising to see Devkota move toward a decidedly pantheistic position.

Rather than in a book I find geometry clearly in Nature, and when I look into the heavens then it's as though the findings of all the astrologers are overturned. I have not acquired as much learning reading volumes as there is in the red and leafy book of the rose, nor as much in all the teachers' exercises as I have found in the pleasing songs flowing over the sand at their own sweet will. Before vast creation man's works of art become dim as moonlight in the day.[48]

He becomes more fully pantheistic while discussing Wordsworth:

Those who say the Universe does not speak are deaf; they are corpses, who maintain that there is no soul in mountains and trees and stars. Philosophers say, even in stones there is the very spirit of Saccidānanda [truth, consciousness, bliss]. . . .[49]

"If there were no rhythm in the universe I could not be a poet."[50] "The beautiful is the fascination of the true."[51] This Keatsian echo is found frequently in Devkota's work and is even translated literally in the poem "Śarad" (Autumn):

> *Sat cha sundarai,*
> *sundarai cha sat.*
>
> The true is the beautiful,
> the beautiful *is* the true.

Society, on the other hand, has taken us away from the truth. Fossilized caste tradition, the lust for possessions, the disregard of spontaneous emotion, all these destroy, drive lovers apart, produce misery and war. At least one of the roots of the problem is education:

The human intellect cannot move hand or foot in the oppression of society's educational system. The teachers are frogs with hollow voices. The obstruction of spontaneous development is termed education. The sandy age of childhood does not want to be held in—what can those poor eager eyes see? Blank, dismal walls. The aim of the instruction of the young is to rid the God-created world of its mysterious magic. We call "books" a mass of nauseating lessons devoid of natural development, ground out, sick and mechanical.[52]

Readers familiar with English Romantic poetry will find little surprising in such attitudes to nature, though they may not appreciate how extraordinarily novel the ideas were for Nepal when the *Essays* were first published in 1945. But in Devkota's work they express only a part of his total attitude. For, reading only a little further in the essays or any of the major poems, we are as likely to find distinctly opposing ideas, such as this from the last essay quoted:

> The tiger eats us so we eat the goat. But humanity begins where the irresponsibility of the beast leaves off. The tiger is only an instrument, there is no fault in *it*.[53]

One thinks of Arnold's "Man must begin, know this, where Nature ends." And although Devkota exculpates the tiger and attributes the human capacity for violence to the way of the world, there is something in the human animal, which must necessarily be a part of nature, that is responsible.

> I understand, there is something poisonous at the root of the world's behavior, some original crookedness, which takes away and obliterates the child's first fear of odious violence.[54]

As the tiger proves, nature is violent. "Where violence ends, eyes and nectar are given to man."[55] Nevertheless, although he may be called a dreamer for it, he would go one step beyond brotherhood with man and declare that he finds "the beginning of civilization in the vibrating of brotherhood with animals and birds and plants."[56]

In *Circe the Enchantress* nature is the enemy which must be fought, first as manifested in the wild sea, then in Circe herself:

> Man's battle-delighting soul
> shows its power against the foe
> and wars with Nature.[57]

22

> Fearfully spoke the lustful Circe:
> Hero, forgive my fault!
> My work is to reveal
> the error of these weak heroes,
> disclose the tempted heart,
> the brute that underlies
> these beastly semblances.[58]

In *Prometheus* the protagonist's triumph is that of the spirit over the physical being, the soul over the beast, civilization over the barbarism of the gods.

> Oh men!
> Vile, mean, sordid souls,
> one step above the apes,
> impoverished animals,
> mouths compelled by Nature's power,
> straws in the wind. . . .[59]

If nature is ambivalent, it is woman who represents the best of it (and surely this accounts, in part, for the preponderance of heroines over heroes throughout Devkota's work).

> The female is righteousness, pity, tenderness,
> the male mere cruelty and brutality,
> only the thirst for power,
> intolerance, the triumphant speech of super-power;
> thunder is the male, terrifying storm of the skies,
> the female, water.
> The father is the great, fearsome brow,
> the mother the pupil of the eye beneath it.[60]

> Father is the bud, mother the life.[61]

In the matter of religion, we have already seen that Devkota is elusive and, very possibly, undecided. If he was really a follower of the Sankhya it could have been only in the loosest sense. Sankhya is, for the most part, non-theistic, but Devkota refers to God (*īśvara, parameśvara*) frequently throughout his work with something more than routine lip-service.

I wish to be separate from the Lord [*paramesvara*] and yet to meet him time after time; otherwise life would be insipid, without the fascination of searching, the tender weeping of separation and the acute bliss of reunion.[62]

In Sankhya the soul, purusha, must learn that it is utterly separate from Nature, prakriti; the entanglements of Nature are the result of illusion, nothing more. The realization of the separateness of the soul from Nature is the primary condition for its liberation *(apavarga, kaivalya)*. Prakriti is dynamic, purusha non-active; the confusion of these two attributes leads to suffering, while the removal of the delusion leads to the cessation of that suffering. There is no *tertium quid,* no interaction of prakriti and purusha, though ignorance deludes us into thinking there is. Sankhya is intellectual, remote from the concerns of ordinary existence (to which it denies importance), and bleak in its conception of salvation, which appears to be an entirely negative conception, not characterized by the ineffable bliss of other Indian systems. It is all in all scarcely the philosophy to have appealed to a poet of Devkota's general temperament, so alive to all the succulent particularities of the everyday world.

At one point in the essays he says:

Finally, I have become a Vedantin. The soul of this fruitful, flowering, colorful, glittering forward-moving song is indeed Creation. My belief inclines toward the idea that the forming of the world was in the immortal vibration of the syllable AUM. For it must truly have been like the rising of the sun! In the soundless solitude of the formless and spotless—the first numb empty silence.[63]

Here, as in many other places in his work, for Devkota the universe-creating *fiat* was sound far more than light, a sound that in its ideal manifestation is still heard as the poet's voice. God himself is the proto-artist: "It is clear as sunshine to me that after [the Creation] the Lord became enchanted by his own love. Love taught the divine sport [*līlā*] and the divine sport produced Creation. The Creation must have been the ritual of his Love." [64]

These are not new ideas in Indian thought—far from it—but it is interesting to see how close to the tradition Devkota comes, iconoclasm and reforming zeal notwithstanding. He defends the sanctity of Krishna against Westerners' attempts to prove him merely a historical or mythological figure: "For me there is the same truth in Vrindavan which Vyasaji proclaimed." [65] And concerning the goddess Sarasvati, patroness of poets and other artists, he writes:

> For me the swan-borne goddess is the truth to the extent that one day, with the consciousness of and belief in that truth, in a dream I held converse with her; she said to me, "Write poetry." I answered, "I don't know how!" Then she herself wrote out, in a handwriting like my late father's, with red letters, a *śloka* [verse], which I immediately memorized. [66]

The bond with India and traditional Indian ideals is frequently alluded to in the essays and poems, [67] and for all his profound love of Nepal, his kinship as an artist, to judge by the essays, is more with the Indian poets Nirala, Pant, and Prasad than with any Nepali contemporaries. [68]

In the curious essay "Five Necessary Things" ("Pāncautā cāhine kurāharū"), God is first, followed by soul, heaven, hell, and *dharma*, for which no single word will do—religion, righteousness, duty, sustaining reality. Here Devkota writes, "The proofs of the existence of God are many. But I am neither a philosopher nor a Vedantin. I argue from matters traced by my own native intellect." [69] "Without God the world is empty. If there is no cause [*kāraṇ*] there is no action [*kārya*]." [70] His final summation is to the effect that "Without God there is no inspiration, without a soul man is clay, there is no ray, no responsibility. Without hell there is no fear and without *dharma* there is no path." [71] The essay is no doubt fanciful, a musing rather than an argument, but it demonstrates the consistent

25

importance of the concept of God in the poet's thinking. Once again, his attitude may best be summed up as an artist's rather than a systematic thinker's.

Philosophy is the elder brother of science, and algebra of Reason. In the philosophicalness of philosophy we see neither truth nor beauty; philosophy is a delusion, poetry is the truth; truth takes its life from the imagination, and that beauty which seems to be the truth and is like the truth, the world of the mind, is so much vaster than the visible universe; in it contact and experiences are fulfilled so much the more in the proximity of truth.[72]

The acceptance of traditional Indian values—the renunciation of the ego,[73] the workings of karma, the transmigration of souls,[74] and the ultimate insubstantiality of the world—"The world is a dream but a divine dream"[75]—permeates his work. In all this he shows himself a believer in the fundamental ideas that pervade all the indigenous Indian religious-philosophical systems. These ideas he finds, ultimately, more in harmony with his own poet's creed than any modern ideology. Faith in emotion and imagination, love of nature, and the quest for a transcendental significance without commitment to a rigorous dogmatism—all are as easily accommodated by the Indian traditionalist as by the Romantic poet. Devkota himself sums it up in one of the most eloquent passages in his prose writings:

Language is a welling up. Grammar must not study the breast filled with the *ras* of heaven but, like it, overflow. It is thus that the natural inspiration of creation resounded for me. . . . Had I been the first living being in an age without language, as soon as I had seen the first roses I could not have remained silent. Words came into being from colors and lines, and afterward came to be called human speech. . . . It seems to me as though the question "Who is it?" (*Ko ho?*) issued from the cuckoo, and the letter "k" [first consonant of the alphabet] is bound up with Nature's first springtime. The heart's own feeling—but I reckon the heart is the first to know it.[76]

The Poetry

He turned the forest colors to ink
and wrote with clean and simple flow;
like the bird he sang in the lovely wood,
in the house, and inside the cage.

("Ghānsī," 1938)

Devkota's creative life can be roughly divided into three major periods. The first, extending through the thirties, includes the sentimental genre poems of *Bhikhārī* (The Beggar, published as a collection for the first time in 1953); the verse drama *Sāvitrī-Satyavān* (1940); and *Munā Madan* (1936), the first of many narrative poems. The second period, the mid-forties, saw the great flowering of Devkota's inspiration in the series of extended narrative poems, among them such works as *Nepālī Śākuntala* (1945), *Sulocanā* (1946), and *Rāvaṇ-Jaṭāyu-Yuddha* (The Battle of Ravana and Jatayu, 1946). The final period begins with the revolutionary poems written in exile in Banaras, reaches its height with the epic *Prometheus* (*Pramithas*, ca. 1950–1951), and includes a vast number of short lyrics, children's poems, and long poems such as "Pāgal" (Crazy, 1953), "Ek Sundarī Veśyāprati" (To a Beautiful Prostitute, 1956), and the various deathbed poems—the poems from inside the cage.

As was noted earlier, the precise dating of many of Devkota's poems, including major works like *Prometheus,* is difficult because of the great gap between the time of composition and the actual date of publication. But the main outline is clear enough, with the peak of the poet's accomplishment represented by the great narrative poems of the mid-forties. The best work of the fifties shows a decline not so much in quality as in sheer scope, although in fact it is my belief that Devkota's imagination and technique both became most original and most expressive in the unrestricted expanse of the narrative poem.

Devkota's first published poem appeared in a 1934 winter issue of the *Gorkhāpatra* [77] under the title "Pūrṇimāko Jaladhi"—"Ocean of the Full Moon." It is rhapsodic and depends very much on alliteration, internal rhymes, and repetitions, along with sanskritized diction and an occasional Hindi word. It is not a good poem, but it is interesting because it stands in such sharp contrast to most of the work that was to follow.

> In the beauty of the full moon
> wildly wildly breaking the depths
> the waves surge, on the shores a language
> clashing clashing,
> the singing of the deep resounds;
> my soul in the wind,
> cresting emotions rise
> in wave after wave,
> the rays the rays
> draw high up the inner torrents,
> shedding the gorgeous foam of bliss,
> tossing tossing
> hurling the ocean over all,
> driving every atom of the water,
> washing and rinsing the darkness in moonlight,
> grand hurly-burly,
> uproar and tumult of the waves,
> in the tumult in the breast
> the singing of the deep resounds
> voicing the unbroken song. [78]

This kind of ecstatic (and in the original mostly unpunctuated) outburst reappears occasionally later, though with somewhat more coherence, as in "Saghan Tamisrāprati" (To a Dark Cloudy Night). In sharp contrast is "Garīb" (Pauper), which appeared only four months later in the spring of 1935 in the first issue of *Śāradā*. [79] This poem also is not distinguished in itself when compared to what was soon to follow, but it is in-

teresting for the simplicity of its language and syntax. This is
not to say that here Devkota has actually begun to write in colloquial Nepali—there is a generous sprinkling of Sanskrit
nouns, though in this respect too it is far more down to earth
than "Ocean of the Full Moon." In thirteen four-line stanzas
Devkota presents a sentimentalized portrait of the pauper and
his life in the form of a monologue. The following stanzas are
typical.

> 1. Poor you say? But you'll find no one
>   anywhere in the world as rich as I.
>   I am no slave to the yearning for luxury,
>   my pleasant labor is sweet to me.
>
> 3. My forehead is beaded with sweat—
>   they're pearls of a price beyond reckoning.
>   A fine lamp of peace is in my house;
>   in every mouthful I eat is the taste of nectar.
>
> 9. My hut is a happy dwelling.
>   You reach it by climbing a stony peak.
>   The winds play unobstructed all about,
>   with the endless blue sky overhead.[80]

And with his imagination—"the fine vehicle of the mind"—he
can cruise the earth, moon, and stars.

Of similar inspiration are other early genre portraits, such
as "Kisān" (The Peasant), 1935; "Ghānsī" (The Grasscutter),
1938; and "Mālī" (The Gardener), 1941—though in this last the
gardener says that the flowers bloom "with the water of tears."

But in "Yātrī" (Pilgrim) and "Bhikhārī" (The Beggar),
both written about 1940 (and both translated in this book), the
tone is different, harsher and more realistic. The beggar's misery is graphically portrayed—in his look is the "silent light of
misery"—while in "Pilgrim" the poet satirizes conventional
religious ideas.[81] In *Munā Madan* the view of poverty is much
less idealized, though the poem contains what is probably
Devkota's most famous tribute to the simple life, lines which
are known by heart by Nepalis of every station:

> Dirty hands and golden plates—
> what can you do with wealth?
> Better to eat greens and nettles
> with a happy heart.

The emphasis in *Munā Madan* is on the conflict of love and money, with real love—charity—usually found in the poorest and humblest.

Devkota's fascination with Wordsworth during this decade is apparent not only in his descriptions of the poor, particularly in terms of the harmony of their lives with nature, but in poems that bear titles like "Samjhanā" (Memory), 1935, and "Bālakkāl" (Childhood), 1938; and, as mentioned earlier, there are long Nepalized versions of "The Solitary Reaper" ("Tinko Ghānsiyā Gīt," i.e., her grass-cutting song), 1935, and "Lucy Gray" (Cāru), 1940.

Devkota's first published book (1936), and still his most popular, was *Munā Madan*. The indebtedness of this romance to Tennyson's *Enoch Arden* has been exaggerated. For all the similarity of the basic plot structure, *Munā Madan* has little in common with Tennyson's once popular narrative, which today seems so insipid and rhetorically inflated. The theme of the separation of lovers, *viraha*, as was pointed out before, is the fundamental stuff of a vast number of Indian literary works of all ages and held for Devkota a special appeal.

In Devkota's simple tale Madan leaves his wife, Muna, to go to Lhasa on business, despite her entreaties not to leave her. Madan stays on in Lhasa while Muna languishes.

> Muna alone, beautiful as the blooming lotus,
> like moonlight touching the cloud's silver shore,
> tender lips parted, her smile showering pearls,
> a flower in December, withering, watered with tears . . .
> long these days, long these nights, sad these days,
> the nights sad whether dark or moonlit,
> Muna at the window, the stars glittering,
>   her dear one in Lhasa,
> tears in her eyes, her heart eaten up with care. . . .[82]

A go-between attempts to bring her together with a would-be lover;

> Six months have passed since your husband went to Lhasa—
> do you really think he hasn't forgotten you with some pretty girl?
> My heart aches to see you abandoned this way:
> the dewdrops of youth stay on the lotus leaf for no one.[83]

Muna indignantly rejects this counsel. In Lhasa Madan finally shakes off his fascination with the city's grandeur and luxury and, with his gold, starts back for Nepal. On the way he comes down with cholera and is abandoned by his companions, then rescued by a Bhote (a Tibetan, or more vaguely any of various Nepali hill peoples of Tibetan origin). This Himalayan Samaritan, who embodies the charity that is to be found in the humblest men, refuses Madan's offer to share his gold.

> What would I do with gold? with wealth?
> Fate plucks it away. These children of mine
> don't eat gold, don't wear jewels—
> my family's on top of the blue sky,
> the clouds their jewels.[84]

Before Madan reaches home his mother falls ill:

> No tears in her eyes filled now with peace,
> light of the end coming into dark waters at evening;
> mainstay of her life, bar to death, her faraway son—
> seeing his face is the trick of her mind as it goes.
> Her thin hand hot with fever, afire with delirium,
> lovingly joins with her daughter-in-law's hand. . . .
> "What's this weeping? don't weep, daughter—
> this is everybody's road, my dear, rich and poor,
> this clay turns to clay and is lost in the sandy shores
>   of grief,
> which you must bear—but not be trapped by it.[85]

Muna's rejected suitor sends her a letter claiming that Madan is dead; before Madan gets back to Kathmandu Muna dies of grief. Madan finds his mother dying—she has survived only long enough to see him once more. His sister tries to calm his frenzied lamentation.

> Be patient, my brother, don't act like this.
> Realize that all must go at last.
> Just a few days for this sinful body, this dirty pride—
> at the end the wind scatters it,
> a handful of ashes, child, a handful of ashes!
> The flower of the flesh withers and goes, mingles with clay,
> but another flower beyond the earth blooms in heaven,
> sways forever in heaven.[86]

Inconsolable, Madan prays for death.

> I won't cry, I'll set out to meet her tomorrow—
> make it fast, O fate! and I'll be grateful to you.[87]

The doctor tries to save him:

> He came, took his pulse—"What medicine,
> tell me, for a sickness of the heart?"[88]

The poem concludes with Madan's death and a little epilogue by the author, who names himself at the end, in the manner of some Sanskrit and *bhakti* poets.

Have you washed the dust from your eyes, brother and sister?
We must understand the world, not let it be a nightmare,
look the world in the face and muster our courage,
while still on the earth move our wings toward the sky.
If to live were mere eating and drinking, what would life be,
    O Lord!
Without a hope of afterlife, what would man be, O Lord!
Still on earth we shall turn our eyes toward heaven—
don't just disappear looking down at the ground.
The mind is the lamp, the body the sacrifice, heaven the grace,
and karma—the worship of God; so says Laxmiprasad.[89]

Munā Madan is written in a popular folk-song meter called *jhyāure*, which had been neglected by poets previously as vulgar and unfit for serious poetry. Devkota begins the poem with an address to the readers.

> How beautiful and sweet our Nepali songs in *jhyāure!*
> this sprout planted unseen in our fields.
> May it bloom and wither, as God wills,
> but grant me this, brother! don't trample it underfoot—
> let it flower and bear fruit! Invite the spring,
> and scorn not the *jhyāure,* dear sir! . . .
> Nepali seed and Nepali grain, the sweet juicy song
> watered with the flavor [*ras*] of Nepal—
> What Nepali would close his eyes to it?
> If the fountain springs from the spirit[90]
> what heart will it not touch?[91]

No doubt it was the combination of the singable (and sometimes singsong) *jhyāure,* the appeal to national feeling, and the attention to local detail, along with the many charming descriptions of Himalayan landscapes, that made *Munā Madan* so popular.[92] In its way it was an epoch-making achievement, a break with the literary past that added a new dimension to Nepali poetry. The simplicity of its emotions and ideals is utterly genuine, though scarcely possible to convey through translation, since it inevitably resides in the poet's diction and the relationship this diction bears to his own earlier poetry as well as contemporaneous literature. *Munā Madan* is only the first of Devkota's many ambitious narrative poems and his first major treatment of *viraha.* The subsequent works are infinitely more complex and subtle, but at their best, as in *Sulocanā,* they recapture the early simplicity, and while they express it with far greater poetic resourcefulness and refinement, they still manage to convey the spring-like naiveté that constitutes the special charm of the earlier work. Not long before he died Devkota is supposed to have said, "It would be right to burn all my works except for *Munā Madan."*

Other important works of this first period are the *Gāine Gīt* (c. 1943), songs in the manner of a now dwindling community of wandering minstrels, and a verse play, *Sāvitrī-Satyavān* (1940), based on the well-known story in the *Mahābhārata* of a wife who, through her devotion to truth, obliges Death to re-

33

store her husband to life.[93] The drama is overextended, but certainly there is eloquence enough in Savitri's dialogues with Death. As so often in the narrative poems the most successful moments are those of the greatest restraint and simplicity of diction, e.g., as when Satyavan, returning to life and unaware of what has happened, says to Savitri:

> I thought I dreamt they carried me to heaven
> and I would not stay
> because I could not find you there.[94]

Another play of the early forties, *Kṛṣi-Bālā* (The Peasant Girl), not published until 1964, is characterized as a "song and dance play." The pastoral world of the lovers Usha and Kiran is darkened by the harsh realities of a landlord's extortion and persecution. After many vicissitudes, Kiran organizes the peasants and forces better terms from the landowner, who in a final gesture of hatred sets fire to the village. *Kṛṣi-Bālā* is rare among Devkota's works for its happy ending. The language in general is extremely down-to-earth and is perhaps the most colloquial to be found anywhere in Devkota's poetry.

Also from this period are three short narrative poems: *Rājkumār Prabhākar* (Prince Prabhakar), a little dream-fable, intended in part to help "cultivate public taste"; *Duṣyanta Śakuntalā Bheṭ* (The Meeting of Dushyanta and Shakuntala), a preliminary study for the *Nepālī Śākuntala,* in which the first meeting of the lovers is described; and *Sītā-Haraṇ* (The Abduction of Sita), relating the episodes from the *Rāmāyaṇa* in which Rama pursues the golden deer and Ravana abducts Sita. This last poem at times suggests an old-style ballad, as in this passage describing Ravana's reaction to Sita's beauty:

> Ravan forgot all his wealth and his people,
>   forgot the very essence of himself,
>   forgot the gleam of Kubera's treasure,
>   forgot the final stroke of death.[95]

Also in evidence are some of those rare passages where Devkota descends to doggerel and worse:

> Oho Rama! Oho Rama!
>   Oho oho oho Rama!
> What a surprise, what a surprise!
>   Where's the golden deer? Where's the golden deer? [96]

The other major works of the early forties are four somewhat more ambitious narrative poems, three of them with contemporary settings and one, *Van Kusum* (Forest Flower, not published until 1968), set in a mythical country that seems modeled on Nepal under the Ranas in the nineteenth century. *Van Kusum* has been criticized on many counts—incorrect Sanskrit usage, too many borrowings from Hindi and even "Hinglish" (*power-vālā!*), distortion of Nepali for metrical purposes, inconsistency in the names of some of the chief characters, and grammatical solecisms. [97] Its plot is complicated and is probably Devkota's most operatic invention, with suicides, disguises, palace conspiracies, and magical drugs that can even bring the dead back to life. All this notwithstanding, the poem makes its satirical point against the Rana oligarchy's oppression and licentiousness. Even more significant is the fact that at the end the hero marries a peasant girl (the Van Kusum of the title), so that intercaste marriage is implicitly sanctioned. The little epic is important as an anticipation of the *Nepālī Śākuntala*, with a brief invocation to Sarasvati, extensive use of diverse classical meters, and a more elaborately developed metaphorical style with a consistent use of color symbolism and imagery derived from water and birds.

By way of contrast, *Mhendu* (first published 1958), *Lūnī* (1967), and *Kunjinī* (1945), all written at about the same time as *Van Kusum,* are purely pastoral, the first two celebrating the life of the hill people who are variously referred to as Tamang, Sherpa, and Bhote. Of *Mhendu* Devkota writes, "In it is the twilit blue enchantment which flowers on the misty slopes up toward Gosainthan. . . . a Nepal here sweetly blending Mongol and Aryan civilizations in an imaginary love story, which. . . . I hope may be heard speaking in the sounds of wild birds and waterfalls."[98] The same might be said of *Lūnī* and *Kunjinī*.

In Devkota's introduction *Mhendu* is termed a *gītikāvya*, a narrative poem in the form of linked short lyrics. Like *Lūnī*, it grew out of Devkota's trek to Gosainthan in 1938. Its story is of the simplest kind. Mhendu ("flower" in Tamang), a girl of Helambu, a mountain district, falls in love with Gumbu, a city boy whom her parents consider a worthless idler, a *guṇḍā*.[99] The lovers defy family and society until Rangja, a sword-wielding tough who is attracted to Mhendu, tries to separate them, threatening them and calling Gumbu a coward. To prove her own courage Mhendu throws herself into the Tadi River and Gumbu follows.

> The waves of the Tadi tell
> > the tale of Mhendu and Gumbu.
> On the shore, they say,
> > Helambu's forest queen is listening.[100]

The story, like that of the other romances, is not logically developed, nor is it meant to be. Its special attractiveness is in the simple and eloquent love songs.

> Where you are
> > there is my home.
> In my soul
> > the voice of your truth.
> In your face
> > the enchantment of God.
> My palace is
> > under your heart,
> the sword of truth
> > under your brows.[101]

In his special introduction for the 1958 edition, Devkota wrote:

> It seems healthy for the poet to seek to move toward popular speech and popular rhythm. How foreign, how far from the world we

have remained in the ivory towers of our epics and lofty poetry! To some degree this "song-narrative" expresses the unstated theory that we should be inclined to bring Nepali literature toward the people and create a form for exploring and revealing the dreams of the people's hearts. . . . *Mhendu* attempts to adapt the style of the English ballad, and the loftiness, and grandeur, and immortality of love is its soul.[102]

Devkota says the theme of the poem is *viyogātmak,* that is, it deals with the sufferings of separated lovers, and expresses the conviction that self-sacrifice is better than violence. "But poems are not made by theories," and if "the waves toss up an oyster, the experts can tell if there are any pearls or not, and how many. We leave the task of disputing and settling the market price to the critics or businessmen. This is an oyster tossed up one day by a whimsical wave."[103]

Though rather longer, *Lūnī,* another *gītikāvya,* is less persuasive, more facile, and often close to doggerel. In this case the heroine is restored to her lover through the good offices of a lama.

Kunjinī took its inspiration from a trip to Jhiltung which Devkota made in 1940 to recuperate from an illness. He had been charmed by the gorges and river valleys of the Mahes, Kolpu, and Trishuli Gandaki, and the scenery figures prominently in the poem. Again the subject is *viyoga,* and the time contemporary with the writing. Kunjini's father will not consent to her marriage to Gorey because he is too poor but relents when Gorey saves Kunjini from drowning in the Kolpu. But before they can be married, Gorey has to leave with his regiment to fight in foreign lands in World War II. While he lies dying in a military hospital, Kunjini's father tries to force her to accept a new, richer suitor. She can find no way to escape except to drown herself in the Kolpu.

Kunjini is one of the most attractive of Devkota's persecuted heroines and foreshadows Sulocana in the poem of that name. As elsewhere in his work the wronged woman is not merely romantic and melodramatically unreal, an excuse for charming lyrics on love and nature. The circumstances of the lives of Kunjini and Mhendu, and of the later Sulocana and Vasanti, are characteristic of the lives of a great many Nepali women even today. In Kathmandu as well as in villages the arranged marriage based on economic considerations (not to mention caste) is the order of the day; falling in love outside the marriage and even love suicides are not unknown. Through his heroines Devkota could criticize social customs and cant, particularly the dichotomy between religious ideals and financial motivations, far more effectively than in his essays. His keen awareness of every kind of social injustice found the most natural vehicle for its expression in the plight of Nepali women. His sympathy was spontaneous, a matter of instinct and conviction, and the lyric mode was its natural voice. Furthermore, through the plot structures of his romances and the vicissitudes of his heroines he was also able to castigate the injustices of the Rana regime with something like impunity during the difficult period of the forties. For Devkota woman had become the most valid and enduring symbol of the Nepali people, so that Kunjini's father and Rangja, the bully who persecutes Mhendu, represent not operatically conventional villains but rather the oligarchy of Ranas and moneyed families who dominated Nepali life. The wonder of this simple allegorization is that so often the poetry is able to bestow credibility and even a poignant beauty on the simple and, for Western readers, threadbare love stories.

Even while he was preoccupied with these romances, Devkota's inspiration had been fed by the ideal of heroic action for both social reforms and the fulfillment of national aspirations. This is reflected in *Kṛṣi-Bālā*, described above, and in *Mahārāṇā Pratāp,* which was completed about 1946, although it was published for the first time in 1967. In this long historical narrative Devkota describes the tribulations of Pratap Singh, Maharana of Mewar, in his struggles against Akbar's invading armies. Apart from Devkota's genuine admiration for the Rajputs, who resisted Muslim domination, he uses the story as a disguised expression of his indignation at the Rana regime. Ironically, the Ranas consider themselves the descendants of the Mewar Rajputs, but in Nepal they are the oppressive invaders.

The much shorter *Rāvaṇ-Jaṭāyu-Yuddha* (The Battle of Ravana and Jatayu) of about the same time (published 1958) is a more original and generally more interesting representation of the heroic ideal. In his introduction Devkota calls the poem a significant attempt to strike out in a new direction, both in his allegorical treatment of the theme and in terms of such technical innovations as free verse, conforming to neither *varṇik* nor *mātrik* meters but rather unlimited in the number of syllables possible in each line.[104] "Feeling and imagination are the rhythm and pulse of poetry, and meter originates from within. . . ."[105]

The poem recounts an incident in the *Rāmāyaṇa* in which the heroic old vulture Jatayu attempts to rescue Sita when Ravana abducts her in his sky-chariot. In Bhanu Bhakta's nineteenth-century version of the *Rāmāyaṇa* the episode is treated in only two stanzas, while in Valmiki the battle is described in 74 verses in the *Forest* canto (*sargas* 50–51). Valmiki's Jatayu is rather prosily moralistic, as may be forgiven one who boasts that he is 60,000 years old, while Bhanu Bhakta's has no personality at all:

Jatayu saw it, flew up and smashed the chariot,
  tore the horses and the bow to pieces.
Ravan, still bolder, swiftly took his sword in hand,
  in a rage cut off both wings and flung them to the ground.
Helpless, Jatayu fell to earth. Then swiftly the villain
  repaired the chariot and, seizing Sita, crossed the sea.[106]

In Devkota's 29-page poem Jatayu is made to represent heroic action based on self-sacrifice in the face of obviously hopeless odds, while Ravana, in whom "there is also a heart," is the monstrous glorifier of material satisfaction. Ravana's lust for the superficial beauty of Sita (whose inner nature he is incapable of discerning) will be paid for in his defeat on the battlefields of Lanka. But even Ravana serves a purpose, Devkota writes: there is a fortune in his depravity, for had he not abducted Sita—"and it would have been unnatural for him not to have coveted so much loveliness . . . the grandeur of her beauty would not have pervaded the world, nor would Rama's valor have been challenged and become worthy of worship."[107] Devkota proceeds to make one of his most explicit esthetic pronouncements: "Valor is in the challenge, not in the victory. Death is the stronger. Believing that the soul of the beautiful is moral, Jatayu regards Ravana's brutality as unnatural and scorns it."[108]

Most astonishing is the fact that these numerous varied works of the forties were no more than incidental music, as it were, for the creation of the poet's masterpieces, *Nepālī Śākuntala* and *Sulocanā*, a staggering instance of prolificness and unflagging inspiration.

Nepalis tend to rank *Nepālī Śākuntala* as Devkota's greatest accomplishment. It is without doubt a remarkable work, a masterpiece of a particular kind, harmonizing various elements of a classical tradition with a modern point of view, a pastoral with a cosmic allegory, Kalidasa's romantic comedy of earthly love with a symbolic structure that points to redemption through the coinciding of sensual and sacred love.

The story is sufficiently well known so that here it is necessary to indicate only those details in which Devkota has departed from Kalidasa's play. The plot follows all the main lines of Kalidasa but developed in epic proportions. Devkota invents a third companion, Charu, for Shakuntala at the hermitage. The lost ring is found not by a fisherman but by the peasant at whose home Shakuntala spends a night on her journey to Dushyanta's court. To justify its title of *Nepālī Śākuntala*, i.e., the Nepali version of the Shakuntala story, the poem is filled with allusions to specifically Nepali flowers and trees, the Himalayas, and so on, and, as Devkota puts it, he creates the "ancient forest in a Nepali home."[109] One Nepali critic justifies the *nepālīpan*, the Nepaliness, of the poem mainly in terms of the freedom and originality of Devkota's treatment.[110] As Bhanu Bhakta had dignified the language by treating the *Rāmāyaṇa* in it, so now Devkota appropriated the brightest jewel of classical Sanskrit drama. A chief element in this originality inheres in the proportions of the plot as Devkota develops it. Most notable is the immense space (some fifty pages, or about 12 percent of the poem) allotted to Menaka's seduction of Vishvamitra, the significance of which will be discussed below. Throughout there are elaborations of ideas and events barely alluded to in Kalidasa—the lovers' gandharva wedding (i.e., without benefit of priest or ritual), Dushyanta's suffering of *viyoga* after he has first met Shakuntala and again after the ring has been found and his memory restored—as well as new episodes or linking passages invented entirely by Devkota, such as Shakuntala's happy dream of the court the night before her departure from the hermitage.

The first stanza of the poem, introducing the invocation, contains the essence of the poem at both human and cosmic levels, wonderfully and—apparently—artlessly compressed:

May Shiva, opening eyes long closed in meditation, see
    the blooming *vasanti* vine dancing to the breeze's
    charming rhythm,
and say, as though he had forgotten, "Tell me who you are"—
        so making Gauri weep,
  then blossoming to a smile bestow a kiss of blessed fortune.[111]

The supreme divine lovers, Shiva and Gauri (Parvati), are shown at the moment when Shiva's jest prefigures what is near-tragic in the lives of Shakuntala and Dushyanta, forgotten love. They represent all nature—the vine that Shiva sees when he opens his eyes is the *vasanti*, also an epithet of the Goddess as the deity of spring *(vasanta)*, so that her identity, or interchangeability with the elements of nature and the seasons (like Shakuntala's), is at once established. As early as Kalidasa Shakuntala is identified with the vine she waters, clinging to the mango-tree, its "husband," in her friend Priyamvada's phrase—it is Priyamvada who sees the resemblance between Shakuntala and the vine.

Devkota's poem may be seen as a pastoral, an evocation of the Golden Age. Significantly set in legendary times, it is one of Devkota's few narratives with a happy ending. (Happy endings apparently struck the poet as incongruous in the age of the Ranas, as *Sulocanā* was soon to demonstrate.) The view of the peasant's life is shown idyllically,[112] again a view very different from the harsh one to be found in *Sulocanā*. The pastoral world is exalted, the court criticized.

> All insipid is the palace, the realms of the crafty,
>   the colors clashing, the city ways cheap.
> Shallow all the glitter, hollow the youthful days there,
>   and our tender flowers twisted on their stems.[113]

As in Kalidasa (and like Shakespeare's Touchstone), the *vidūṣaka*, the Brahman jester,[114] makes a good case against country life in his satirical outbursts.[115] Just as in *As You Like It* there is a double irony, for the Arcadian world, despite all its charms, cannot suffice in itself; ultimately, the Golden Age ceases to be a matter of geography. But when the *vidūṣaka* criticizes the forest girls Dushyanta corrects him: "These flowers are wild ones, natural, blooming with the beauty of vines, and free of city fickleness."[116] And Shakuntala's innocence, like Miranda's in *The Tempest*, is so complete that when she first sees Dushyanta she asks, "Is he a man or a *kinnar*, a deity or Māra [Kāma]?"[117]

As in Shakespearean romance, reconciliation is the goal. Even the two hostile goddesses of art and wealth are finally at peace with one another: "Lakshmi dwelt now in harmony with Sarasvati."[118] Other opposites are fused together in Shakuntala herself:

> She, part celestial nymph and part royal,
>   wanders taking earth and heaven together;
> scorning the bliss of sages' austerities,
>   like bliss incarnate she takes new heaven.[119]

It would be tedious to cite all the identifications of human and divine and human and natural throughout the poem. Although the human dimension of Devkota's characters is never lost (as Gautami's stern sermon on conjugal love reminds us before Shakuntala begins her journey to court), he is aiming at a vast allegory of love, nature, and civilization, as a few examples will make clear.

With the brevity of human happiness well in mind,[120] Devkota does not hesitate to attribute the character of a universal sacrament to the gandharva wedding of the lovers—spring is the priest, the sky the canopy, the birds the ceremonial musicians. Dushyanta even says, "We two shall be the sun and moon."[121] (Typically, there is an allusion to the fact that he is of the lunar race.) The terrestrial paradise of their first encounter cannot endure, but it will be replaced by a genuine paradise for their reunion, a paradise they will presumably take with them even when they return to earth.

In the conventional allegory of the Sankhya philosophy, which as we have noted held a particular interest for Devkota, nature *(prakṛti)* is feminine while the soul *(puruṣa)* is masculine, and in fact the word also may simply denote a human male. This is the reverse of the more conventional sentimental humanism Devkota demonstrates in so much of his work. He deals with this paradox most explicitly in the beginning of his *Śākuntala* in the treatment of his heroine's parentage. The man who is to be her father, Vishvamitra, most austere and powerful of sages, an awesome human embodiment of spirit triumphing over the flesh, is entangled and brought low by a creature from the spirit realm, Menaka, who despite her origin manifests all too plainly earthly sensuality. Their child will be human, female, and spiritually pure, while her lover is selfish, sensual, and cruel (whether consciously or not), so that in this second generation the old humanistic pairings are once more symbolically aligned in opposition to the Sankhya symbology. As in the late romances of Shakespeare, nature is redeemed by the innocence of the daughter. Furthermore, Menaka, while performing what is apparently a selfish and destructive act (Indra has commanded her to seduce Vishvamitra to prevent his gaining ascendance over the gods), restores the sage, if only temporarily, to the realm of human feeling. Reversing the pattern, Shakuntala will be the redemptive instrument of Dushyanta's ennoblement and the means whereby he recognizes his oneness with nature. The deer he pursues becomes Shakuntala; and she, as a queen of nature, redeems both the natural fault which is her origin and then, through separation from Dushyanta, him as well. At the point when the ring is found and her lover's memory is restored, he becomes a fit instrument for the work of the gods and can lead their forces to victory over the demons. In this way the human ascendance which Indra, as chief of the gods, had feared in Vishvamitra is attained by Dushyanta through the influence of the sage's daughter—for without a human ally the gods would go down to defeat.

So much might be inferred in Kalidasa's drama, but in Devkota's version the allegorical elements are explicitly developed to the point where they provide the true subject of the poem. Both Kalidasa's celebration of the family and the old romantic convention of the pathetic fallacy are transformed into a kind of cosmic analogue for the ultimate harmony of a universe in which nature and civilization are perfectly fused and sustained by love.

It should not be forgotten that even in this romantically spiritual epic Devkota has remained true to his liberal ideals: Shakuntala is as much a wronged heroine as her more commonplace sisters in the poet's other narrative works, and the allusions to the Ranas are plain enough. Rejected by Dushyanta, Shakuntala threatens him with a prophecy of revolution and a new order. "Calling yourself a king, you oppress all people unjustly. . . . this throne will shake. . . . The fortresses will crumble on the black path of unrighteousness," and so on.[122] Nevertheless, the main emphasis of the poem is on the gospel of love, as enunciated in the rishi's valediction to the lovers near the end of the poem—lines that could stand as an epigraph for all Devkota's work:

> Love is the first order of creation—know this, the
> foundation of the universe.
> Love is the honeyed compassion of divinity; love is
> the breath of the universe.
> Love attains the stars—know this, the principle of
> everybody's *dharma*.
> To scorn it is a sin, know this, O king: this love
> is the divine song.[123]

Nepali critics, while heaping praises on Devkota's *Śākuntala*, have nevertheless pointed to shortcomings which have come to be regarded as typical of his work and which he himself cites:[124] obscurity, faults in the classical meters, solecisms and stylistic oddities, and over-sanskritization.[125] But there is no doubt that the quality of the poem is sustained prodigiously and, despite the rapidity of its composition, technique and melodic charm falter but rarely. The *Nepālī Śākuntala* represents a kind of apotheosis of Devkota's love for the classical Indian tradition. From this point on in his career his attention was to be almost entirely given to the present-day world. The one notable exception, *Prometheus*, is a timeless allegory as well as a baleful prognostication of its author's own destiny.

Sulocanā at first glance seems much like the earlier romances, except for its great length (15 cantos, 312 pages). But even a casual perusal reveals that it is of quite a different order.

The whole first canto is devoted to an elaborate invocation

to various divinities, and the second to the somewhat fanciful genealogy of Sulocana's family before it settled in Kathmandu. In a vague place and time, the founder of the family, a Kshatriya, repenting his killing of a deer (a conscious echo of the Sanskrit epics), builds a temple and founds a petty kingdom on the banks of the Ganges. His descendants, like Devkota's ancestors, move their residence to Devkut in Western Nepal (occasion for a splendid descriptive hymn of praise for the beauty of the country) and a generation later move on to Kathmandu where Sulocana and her brothers, Chand Mardan and Timir Mardan, are born, the children of Shatru Mardan Singh, a World War I hero, and his wife, Makhna.

But from the end of the second canto on it is clear that this is not a conventional romance when a classical Sanskrit meter is used to inform the reader that Shatru Mardan has lost an eye in the war, or to convey such facts as:

The two brothers eagerly studied English together
and they got their B. A. Pass in the year '95 [1938].[126]

In his introduction Devkota writes that the work might be a *mahākāvya*, an epic, in name only. "In this work I may be a poetic dramatist or a novelist in verse."[127] The poem is built of "common social novelistic materials."[128] And indeed it is filled with minute observation of contemporary upper-middle-class Kathmandu society. The poet had written a fragment of a "social novel," as he called it, *Campā*, in the early forties, and many of the realistic short stories belong to this period, as well as the humorous and genre-description essays ("Gambling," "Moustaches," "The Bengali Doctor's Skinny Jackass"). But characteristically only in verse was he able to give full expression to that domain which provides other writers with the material for the naturalistic novel. The formal meters— *anuṣṭubh, śārdūlavikrīḍita* etc.—are made to convey minutiae of dress, furniture, and eating as naturally as for other poets they served their more conventional function of expressing every sort of emotional and esthetic refinement.

This is not to say that the Romantic elements disappear, for they continue to abound—the praise of love, ideal devotion, complete self-sacrifice; but for the most part they are treated with greater success than in the earlier poems and harmonized with the realistic setting.

In childhood Sulocana and Anang were friends until their fathers began feuding over a dice game. Years later, at school Anang becomes friends with Sulocana's brothers. On his way home from their house late one night he comes upon Sulocana singing in the garden. They fall in love and after this meet again with Sulocana's brothers. On this occasion a fierce debate springs up over the existence of God, Chand Mardan and Timir Mardan holding forth as atheists while Sulocana and Anang defend their conviction that God exists. As Anang says:

Our God flashes by means of the heart to the heart,
calling with mysterious resonance through the curtain of *viyoga*. [129]

Placed almost casually in Anang's long statement, the reference to *viyoga* is the first hint of Devkota's favorite theme and the fated course of the story. Shatru Mardan bursts in and in a rage throws Anang out. Soon after this Sulocana is betrothed to Vilas Singh, a much older man, dissolute and ugly. Before the marriage Sulocana desperately pleads her cause, in lines that are among the most famous in all Devkota's work:

> Only one time blooms the rose
> with the tender warmth of the ray.
> The blossom does not turn to a bud again—
> time shakes it down before the world.
>
> Everyone has but one heart—
> it opens with one sun for a day.
> Only one moon rules the night;
> only one image keeps fresh forever. [130]

47

Unable to move her father and mother, she plans to elope with Anang. But, stricken with smallpox, he fails to meet her, and her marriage to Vilas Singh is hastily solemnized. She is rejected by her husband, who takes a second wife more to his liking, and her mother-in-law reviles and abuses her. Her only friend is her widowed sister-in-law, Bijuli, a high-spirited and rebellious girl who intends to enjoy her widowhood:

> ". . . I have a right
> to enjoy my youth. Why should I hold back?
>
> When I see some fine good-looking young fellow
> I signal with my eyes—that's my nature." [131]

When Bijuli becomes pregnant by one of the house servants (who quickly disappears), her mother sends her away to the house of one of their tenant farmers in Sundarijal to have her baby. Here Timir Mardan, who had earlier been attracted to her, finds her and befriends her; feeling sorry for her at first, he quickly falls in love with her.

In Kathmandu Sulocana has withdrawn completely into herself except for her devotion to Lord Krishna, which, as Timir points out with his characteristic modernity of outlook, is only a sublimation of her sexual frustration. A new servant comes to work for the family, Jaimane, Anang in disguise. He builds a little shrine to Krishna for Sulocana and often in the evening plays the flute—these are the only consolations in her bleak married life. One night Vilas Singh, incited by his second wife, bursts into Sulocana's room, searches through her effects and finds a letter from her to Anang. Wild with jealousy he begins to beat her savagely and orders her out of the house. At this point Jaimane runs in and pleads with Vilas to allow Sulocana to stay at least this night. He tells everything about Sulocana's earlier life, her two meetings with Anang, and her innocence, and then disappears just as Sulocana has recognized him. Vilas Singh relents and later that night, stricken with conscience, aware that he has destroyed the happiness of two people, shoots himself.

Ill with consumption, Sulocana is taken to Pashupatinath to die. Here Bijuli and Timir Mardan visit her, provoking her only smile, and then a strange-looking man, who can be called "neither madman nor sage," Anang in his last disguise, appears just as Sulocana dies.

Elements from the earlier romances are readily distinguishable in this brief plot summary, but *Sulocanā* stands apart from them not only by virtue of its much greater scope and the dense accumulation of social and political details, but also by reason of its generally tight organization and the sharp psychological analysis that supports the characters' motivations. If at moments the melodramatic climaxes, so typical of the earlier poems, seem to clash with the naturalistic and psychological tone, it should be remembered that Devkota is not part of a Western tradition (no matter how important the influence of the West on his work may be), nor, for that matter, is there any clear Indic tradition behind his work in this form. In the narrative poems he is authentically *sui generis,* creating quite new vehicles for the expression of his thought. The moments of high melodrama sweep one along by their eloquence and conviction, so that one is quite willing to suspend disbelief for the moment, just as in certain nineteenth-century operas one is moved by the power of the music and the fundamental truth of the universal emotions to accept—or not even to notice—the extravagant theatricality of the dramatic action. And as has been noted before, both the unexpectedly violent act and the public (and lengthy) outpouring of intense emotion are far from strange to everyday life in the Kathmandu Valley.

Also analogous to romantic operatic convention is the use of the set piece, the elaborately developed *scena,* as it were, in the form of aria or ensemble. In *Sulocanā* Nepalis respond with particular warmth to the long lyric set pieces on love or *viyoga*, religious fervor, denunciation, or justification.

There is a vague underlying allegorical structure in *Sulocanā*. The significance of some of the characters' names bears this out. Sulocana herself ("the girl with the beautiful eyes") is a personification of ideal innocence and beauty destroyed by hypocritical social convention and ossified traditions. Her father is paradoxically named Shatru—enemy—and her lover Anang—"bodiless," an epithet of Kāma, the Hindu Eros, but here ironically also indicative of Anang's ultimate ineffectuality and his passive capacity to suffer (like Madan, another epithet of Kāma, in *Munā Madan*). Vilas, "luxury" or "philandering," and Bijuli, "lightning," are obvious enough, and it is Bijuli who humanizes the rather drily intellectual Timir, "darkness."

From the beginning of the work it is emphasized that Shatru Mardan's ancestors were petty rajas far to the South in India, and that today the family's pride is excessive, incommensurate, certainly, with its relative unimportance in the twentieth century. Apart from lineage and wealth these people have no claim to distinction, either in the esthetic or in the moral sphere, as they demonstrate with their brutal treatment of Sulocana, she being in effect the human sacrifice they insist on making to their own absurd notion of themselves. Their hostility to Anang's family stems from much more than the gambling dispute. Anang is a *khatrī*, born of a Brahman father and a Kshatriya mother. The abuse Shatru and Anang's father hurl at one another is mostly along caste lines, untranslatable in large part because Nepali is rich in abusive epithets referring to caste and meaningless to those outside the system.[132] And just as Shatru Mardan represents a self-important and obsolescent autocracy (the Ranas), so Anang's father stands for the hypocritical and parasitical community of those Brahmans who wield a power far out of proportion to either their intelligence or their moral integrity. Both classes are the enemies of love, spontaneous and honest feeling, general human decency, and even common sense. Their power is destructive where it should be sustaining, according to both natural familial bonds and the religious precepts they proclaim. Sulocana and Anang are far too fragile to persevere against them, but Bijuli and Timir Mardan are not: by falling in love in the unacceptable modern way and then by living together they affront the tradition of marriage and, worse, that of the suppressed, near-invisible role a widow is expected to play.

In the tradition of Sanskrit literature there is theoretically no room for tragic endings, and in practice they scarcely ever occur. If *viyoga* is an almost inevitable element of the dramatic substance of both drama and classical *kāvya*, it is also true that such separation is expected just as inevitably to conclude with the reunion of the parted lovers. The drama and *kāvya* constantly allegorize the cyclical nature of human experience, the renewal of the seasons and of time itself, and the potential (and ultimate) harmony of all the workings of the universe. By dealing in his romances with *viyoga* as a situation tragic because it is, as it were, irreversible, Devkota departs strikingly from the tradition with which he was so imbued. The characteristically modern note of tragic irreconcilability, not surprising in itself, is startling in the traditional Indian contexts Devkota provides for it. In his work *Sulocanā* is the apotheosis of the tale saturated in *viyoga* led to a desperately pessimistic conclusion.

Sulocanā makes an interesting companion piece for the *Nepālī Śākuntala*, the latter celebrating a traditional glory and the former castigating the decadence and cruelty of a modern Hindu kingdom. Both dramatize the cause of the wronged woman and her vindication, one as an epic set in legendary times, the other set among tragic realities of the present day. Each is remarkable for its conviction and intensity, and together they may be said to represent the height of Devkota's poetic achievement.

While in exile in Banaras Devkota apparently became fascinated with Greek mythology. Of the five narrative poems of this period, two—*Vasantī* and *Mainā,* short song-narratives in *jhyāure,* both published in 1952—have Nepali subjects. The others are *Māyāvinī Sarsī* (Circe the Enchantress, published 1967), *Sundarī Projerpinā* (The Fair Prosperina, published 1952) and *Pramithus* (Prometheus, published 1971).

Whether or not this interest in the Hellenic tradition sprang from Devkota's quest to find new analogues to express his criticism of the Rana regime, the scope of the poems is much broader than the nationalistic fervor which informed *Mahārāṇā Pratāp,* to say nothing of the revolutionary poems of the same period of exile, occasional pieces marked by propagandistic sermonizing and slogan-making. *Prometheus,* Devkota's final experiment with epic poetry, is particularly significant as a synthesis of the poet's democratic humanism with the esthetic moralism that so strongly characterized his sense of the poet's vocation; both these elements are electrified by his own intense experience of personal suffering.

Prometheus, though it ends at approximately the same point as Aeschylus' drama, is closer in spirit to Shelley. There is, for instance, no suggestion (as in the Greek work) that for all his heroic opposition to Zeus and his immense benefaction of humankind, Prometheus is nevertheless guilty of hubris. The action of the poem spans the whole story of Gaea and her children, the Titanomachy, Prometheus's civilizing mission to the world of men, and his punishment by Zeus, and ends with Hermes' unsuccessful attempt to reconcile Prometheus with Zeus, with the ensuing rending of the earth

> as though the cosmic panther,
> shaped of blackness, to swallow up all earth
> gaped with the bestial mouth of the vast.[133]

As in the case of the *Nepālī Śākuntala,* Devkota makes only minor changes from the traditional story. Io is omitted, while the Daughters of Okeanos, as consoling as those in Aeschylus, also summon a group of goddesses—Freedom, Hope, Beauty, the Arts, and Love—to comment and prophesy, with Beauty recounting the future wars provoked by Helen in the West and Sita in the East. Devkota emphasizes the altruism and heroism of Prometheus, his compassion for mankind, and his stoic willingness to bear an all-too-human suffering. "Promethean pain I bear," Devkota was to begin his final poem in English a few days before his death, continuing, "Yet a song of joy must I raise," while Prometheus, bearing human pain, after his first night of torment on the rock in the Caucasus, greets the dawn with a magnificent hymn of praise to Apollo. Devkota also speaks of the oppressive regime in Nepal in the course of the work and raises a cry for revolutionary change, but it seems fanciful to cite such lines as the following, as some critics have done, as Marxist:

Rise armed against the darkness, O man,
Die deriding the darkness in the red or white heat,
Take on the awareness of immortality, rise up against heaven:[134]

As in the other narrative poems, there are set pieces, invocations, arguments, and hymns of praise, such as the one to Apollo mentioned above and one to fire, which has an almost Vedic ring to it:

> Hail! Thou art the god of fire,
> O giver of universal life, creator of the jungle,
> destruction of the forest, shaper and dissolver thou!
> thou nourishment of all the world.[135]

There are also occasional echoes of Murray's translation of *Prometheus Unbound*, as Joshi has pointed out,[136] and possibly of Shelley and Wordsworth as well. All in all, the sense of Nepalization is much less apparent than in the *Śākuntala,* and one wonders if Devkota was consciously aiming at a more universal poetry in which the two great traditions that he knew could be synthesized harmoniously. Certainly, no other writer of the subcontinent has dealt with Western classical material with such ambition and such conviction.

The poems that follow *Prometheus* tend to be more intimate and subjective, even before the lyrics that relate specifically to the writer's final illness. Although the obscurities continue, there is less sanskritization, and the material relates more immediately to the poet's experience and to the contemporary life of Nepal without benefit of allegory or transmutation through myth or tradition. Some of the best of these poems appeared in the six issues of *Indrenī* (1956), which was edited by Devkota—poems like "Pāgal" (Crazy), "Dāl-Bhāt-Ḍukū" (Beans and Rice and Mustard Greens) and "Bhūtlāī Jhaṭāro" (Beat the Ghost). This is also the time of the children's poems of *Sunko Bihāna* (Golden Morning), published in 1953, and the 1958 collection of humorous verse entitled *Manoranjan* (Entertainments), not published until 1967. Even in this essentially light verse the dark note rings unexpectedly, as in the poem called "Palṭan" (The Battalion), a conventional patriotic poem:

> Clay is this body,
> it flies up and turns to wind.[137]

Or later in the same poem:

> The body becomes dust and goes,
> only the soul will bloom.[138]

The final poems in Nepali from the last weeks at Shanta Bhavan give every evidence of a trend toward more personal speech, intense and even stark:

> Like sand in a vast desert I am hot,
> I burn, dying without hope, dumb,
> I am empty as a dried-up tree . . .[139]

This represents the final purgation of the long-lived Romantic spirit in Devkota's works. These last poems suggest strongly that the poet had not ceased growing and had begun to move toward a radically new phase in his development. What precisely it would have been we can only speculate upon, but to judge from the poems of September 1959, the darkening of the spirit would have shone forth with an ever surer clarity of utterance.

A Note on the Translation

The translator of Devkota must confront a multitude of formidable problems.

There is first of all the unpredictable originality of the poet's mind and the frequent obscurity of his diction. Furthermore, manuscripts are not always legible, and often his Nepali editors will not even hazard a guess as to how to read a word or whole line.

The poor standard of Nepali printing is a further complication. In those cases where one is fortunate enough to have two or more different printings of the same poem, the texts rarely tally exactly, even to the point of lines and whole stanzas missing from a particular version. Syllabic division may come at different points, utterly changing the meaning, or a dot (indicating nasalization) may be left out, changing a verb without a clarifying pronoun from the first person plural to the second. The letters *ḍ* and *u* are often mistakenly set for one another, so that in different printings of "Beans and Rice and Mustard Greens," for example, one has a choice of *ḍarbāṭa* or *urbāṭa*, "from fear" or "from the breast (heart)." The latter is most likely correct, but the former is not impossible. Most of the difficulties the translator encountered in the poems taken from *Bhikhārī* disappeared with the printing of a new edition carefully corrected by the poet's son, but this painstakingly edited volume is unique among editions of Devkota.

Then there is Devkota's enormous vocabulary, with words slipped in from Newari, Tamang, and even Tibetan, to say nothing of a great number of dialect words from various parts of Nepal. To refer again to "Beans and Rice and Mustard

Greens," the word *rauśiera* is used; it is not to be found in any dictionary of Nepali, though it seems to be generally understood by educated people. The verb *rauśinu,* to become excited, is a dialect word from the eastern districts of Nepal.

Furthermore, there is the question of which poems can be translated at all without the laborious machinery of extensive footnote commentary to make them understandable to an audience that does not consist of either Hindus or professional Indologists.

Along with the difficulties of the actual translation, the translator of a poet like Devkota, especially his first translator, is faced with the problem of what poems to choose. The *oeuvre* is immense and inexhaustibly various. There is the additional complication that the poet's finest work, at least in this translator's opinion, is represented by his long narrative poems, e.g., *Sulocanā, Prometheus,* and *Nepālī Śākuntala,* as well as the shorter but still extensive romances such as *Mhendu* and *Kunjinī.* With very rare exceptions it seems pointless to select excerpts from these works, since the quality of any passage is inextricably bound up with its significance in the coherence of the whole poem.

Whatever the faults of this attempt at translating some of Devkota's poems, I hope that it will stimulate the further study of his work and new, more skillful translations, perhaps even of the major narrative poems in their entirety. And beyond this—since almost all the Americans and Europeans who have studied Nepali in recent years have been interested in the language only as an aid to field research in religion and the social sciences—that there may be some kindling of interest in the other literature of Nepal, an interest which is richly merited. Finally, implicit in this enterprise has been the wish that admirers of Nepal, loveliest of mountain kingdoms, may gain a new insight into the land and its people from this sampling of poetry which has sprung so spontaneously and so generously from the heart of the country.

Notes to the Introduction

1. On the history of Nepali see T. W. Clark, "Nepali and Pahaṛi," in *Current Trends in Linguistics*, vol. V, *Linguistics in South Asia*, ed. Thomas A. Sebeok (Leiden: Mouton, 1969), pp. 253 ff., and T. W. Clark, "The Rani Pokhri Inscription, Kathmandu," *Bulletin of the School of Oriental and African Studies* (1957), 20:184–85.

2. For the relationship of Bhanu Bhakta to his sources, see Mathuradatta Pandey, *Nepālī aur Hindī ke Bhakti-kāvya kā Tulnātmak Adhyayan* (Delhi: Bharatiy Granth Niketan, 1970.)

3. There is very little in English on these writers. See Ishwar Baral, "Balkrishna Sama," *Kailash* (1974), vol. 2, no. 3. Some observations of Devkota on these contemporaries of his may be found in Appendix I, "Devkota on Devkota."

4. See Appendix I. The essay was not published until 1970, eleven years after his death.

5. A slightly different version is given by some sources: "Know the sea of deep sorrow, brother—never be proud—we must die." See Svayambhulal Shresta, "Mahākavi Devkoṭā: Saṃkṣipta Jīvanī ra Kehī Saṃsmaraṇ," *Bhānu* (1963), 5:183–84.

6. L. P. Devkota, *Lakṣmī Nibandha Saṅgrah* (Kathmandu: Sajha Prakashan, 1962), p. 62. This collection of Devkota's Nepali essays will be referred to hereafter as *Essays*. All translations from the *Essays* are mine.

7. Ibid., p. 64.

8. Ibid., p. 65.

9. Since 1845 the king had ruled only in name, actual power being vested in the hands of the prime minister, who was always a member of one of a few interrelated Rana families. The king recovered his authority in the revolution of 1950–1951.

10. There was no university in Nepal until 1959.

11. For much of Devkota's work it is difficult to assign precise dates of composition. Many poems and prose pieces were published posthumously, others during his lifetime but years after they had been written. Kumarbahadur Johsi has established an approximate chronology, given in his study of Devkota's major narrative poems, *Mahākavi Devkoṭā ra Unkā Mahākāvya* (Kathmandu: Sahyogi Prakashan, 1975), which I have in general followed.

12. *Essays*, p. 104.

13. Ibid., p. 102.

14. Quoted in Janaklal Sharma, *Mahākavi Devkoṭā: Ek Vyaktitva, Duī Racanā* (Kathmandu: Sajha Prakashan, 1975), pp. 25–26. Sharma has a quite dif-

ferent interpretation of the "geographical mistake": he believes the doctor was merely expressing the inevitable European view that a man of genius had to be essentially European and not Asian (ibid., pp. 26–27).

15. Ibid., p. 107.

16. *Essays*, p. 13.

17. Quoted in Nityaraj Pande, *Mahākavi Devkoṭā* (Lalitpur: Madan Puruskar Guthi, 1960), p. 27.

18. Sharma, *Mahākavi Devkoṭā*, pp. 25–26.

19. N. Pande, *Mahākavi Devkoṭā*, p. 30.

20. For many details concerning the last weeks of Devkota's life I am indebted to Dr. Miller, who kindly allowed me to read the chapters on Devkota from his unpublished book on his nine years' service in Nepal.

21. The poet's family has kindly made this private tape-recording available to me; it is scarcely necessary to stress its immense value, not only for the factual information it contains, but especially for the poet's living voice, his pronunciation of both English and Nepali, and his style of reading or reciting his work in both languages.

22. Tape-recorded conversation, September 11, 1959.

23. Ibid., September 4.

24. Ibid., September 11.

25. Quoted by N. Pande, *Mahākavi Devkoṭā*, p. 62.

26. Personal communication from Dr. Miller.

27. N. Pande, *Mahākavi Devkoṭā*, p. 62.

28. In a chapter of his travel memoir *Gone Away* (Boston: Little, Brown, 1960), entitled "Dying Poet," the Indo-Anglian poet Dom Moraes describes a visit he paid, along with Ved Mehta, an American journalist of Indian origin, to Devkota at Pashupatinath during one of the last two days of his life. As journalistic observation it is superficial, not to say silly, but has some value in that it records (although one cannot be sure how accurately) some of Devkota's comments during the last hours of his life.

29. Reported in Moraes, *Gone Away*, p. 137.

30. *Essays*, p. 105.

31. Moraes, *Gone Away*, p. 148.

32. The view of Madhusudan Devkota, a brother of the poet, expressed in a personal communication. See also N. Pande, *Mahākavi Devkoṭā*, pp. 166 ff.

33. Jagdish Ghimire, *"Dvandātmak Bhautikvādī Prometheus,"* *Bhānu* (1963), 5:194–208.

34. Mohanraj Sharma, *"Mahākavi Lakśmīprasād Devkoṭā: Vyakti ra Kṛti,"* in Laxmiprasad Devkota, *Māyāvinī Sarsī* (Varanasi: Nepali Sahitya Ghar, 1967), pp. 9–15.

35. *Essays*, p. 195.

36. E.g., *Rāmāyaṇa* and the story of Shakuntala (both favorite subjects of

Devkota, which he treated in many different works), the Nala and Damyanti romance from the *Mahābhārata,* the *Gīta Govinda,* and a large proportion of the vernacular poetry of Vidyapati, Tulsi, and others.

37. *Essays,* p. 142.
38. Ibid., p. 141.
39. Ibid., p. 123.
40. Ibid., p. 94.
41. Ibid., p. 97.
42. Ibid., p. 21.
43. Ibid., p. 223.
44. Ibid., p. 201.
45. Ibid., p. 87.
46. Ibid., p. 19.
47. Ibid., p. 44.
48. Ibid., p. 142.
49. Ibid., p. 110.
50. Ibid., p. 144.
51. Ibid., p. 142.
52. Ibid., pp. 240–41.
53. Ibid., p. 228.
54. Ibid., p. 225.
55. Ibid., p. 228.
56. Ibid., p. 230.
57. L. P. Devkota, *Māyāvinī Sarsī,* p. 12.
58. Ibid., pp. 65–66.
59. L. P. Devkota, *Pramithus* (Kathmandu: Nepal Rajkiy Pragya-Pratisthan, 1971), p. 34.
60. Ibid., p. 22.
61. Ibid., p. 23.
62. *Essays,* p. 147.
63. Ibid., p. 146.
64. Ibid., p. 147.
65. Ibid., p. 167.
66. Ibid.
67. See *Essays,* pp. 167, 181–82, and the great number of major poems based on Indian mythological subjects.
68. See *Essays,* pp. 109, 111, 150, 182.
69. Essays, p. 39.
70. Ibid., p. 38.
71. Ibid., p. 43.
72. Ibid., p. 166.
73. Ibid., pp. 196, 199.

74. Ibid., pp. 197 ff.

75. Ibid., p. 207.

76. Ibid., pp. 143–44.

77. The Nepali date is v.s. 15 Mārg *gate* 1991.

78. Quoted in N. Pande, *Mahākavi Devkoṭā*, pp. 12–13.

79. v.s. Phalgun 1991.

80. L. P. Devkota, *Bhikhārī* (Kathmandu: Sajha Prakashan, 1974), pp. 33–35.

81. L. P. Devkota, *Munā Madan* (Kathmandu: Sajha Prakashan, 1970), p. 3.

82. Ibid., p. 14.

83. Ibid., p. 17.

84. Ibid., p. 38.

85. Ibid., pp. 39–40.

86. Ibid., p. 49.

87. Ibid., p. 51.

88. Ibid.

89. Ibid., p. 52.

90. *Pratibhā* could also be translated "true genius."

91. *Munā Madan*, facing p. 1.

92. For a few years now a musical setting of portions of the poem, performed as an opera, has been selling out all performances through the winter season in Kathmandu.

93. In J. A. B. van Buitenen's translation of the first three volumes of the *Mahābhārata*, this episode is found in vol. 2 (Chicago: University of Chicago Press, 1976), pp. 760–78.

94. L. P. Devkota, *Sāvitrī-Satyavān* (Kathmandu: Sajha Prakashan, 1967), p. 99.

95. L. P. Devkota, *Sītā-Haraṇ* (Kathmandu: Sajha Prakashan, 1967), p. 35.

96. Ibid., p. 15.

97. See Kamal Dikshit's Introduction to *Van Kusum* (Kathmandu: Sajha Prakashan, 1968), pp. 9–11.

98. L. P. Devkota, *Mhendu* (Kathmandu: N. Bh. Pr. Samiti, 1958), p. *k*.

99. Not necessarily a hoodlum, as in Hindi, but rather a dissolute playboy in Kathmandu usage.

100. *Mhendu*, p. 29.

101. Ibid., p. 18.

102. Ibid., pp. *k–kh*.

103. Ibid., p. *kh*.

104. For further comment on Devkota and classical meters see Appendix I.

105. L. P. Devkota, *Rāvaṇ-Jaṭāyu-Yuddha* (Kathmandu: N. Bh. Pr. Samiti, 1958), p. *k*.

106. Bhanu Bhakta, *Āth-Kaṇḍ-Rāmāyaṇ* (Varanasi: B. M. Sharma, 1970), p. 66.

107. *Rāvan-Jaṭāyu-Yuddha,* p. *kh*.

108. Ibid., p. *g*.

109. L. P. Devkota, *Nepālī Śākuntala* (Kathmandu: Sajha Prakashan, 1968), p. 3.

110. Joshi, *Mahākavi Devkoṭā ra Unkā Mahākāvya,* p. 92.

111. *Nepālī Śākuntala,* p. 1.

112. Ibid., pp. 288 ff.

113. Ibid., p. 173.

114. A stock character in classical Sanskrit drama, companion to the hero.

115. *Nepālī Śākuntala,* pp. 146 ff.

116. Ibid., p. 167.

117. Ibid., p. 153. *Kāma* is the Indian Eros; a *kinnar* is a mythical creature, with a human body and a horse's head.

118. Ibid., p. 88.

119. Ibid., p. 87.

120. As on p. 251: "Nature grants no lasting joy of life,/Spring holds but brief sway in our seasons. . . ."

121. *Nepālī Śākuntala,* p. 252.

122. Ibid., pp. 360 ff.

123. Ibid., p. 440.

124. See Appendix I, "Devkota on Devkota."

125. Here is an example of this last for readers of Sanskrit (from p. 9):

suna miṣṭakathā subhāṣinī
    mṛdumādhuryavilāsamohinī
vanaśitalavārivāhinī
    śivasatsundaratāninādinī.
suna kovidakālidāsako
    kalakallolakalasvalaṁkṛtā
racanāpratibimbinī kathā
    saba yo bhāratako priya-jyathā.

126. L. P. Devkota, *Sulocanā* (Kathmandu: Sajha Prakashan, n.d.), p. 40.

127. Ibid., Introduction, p. 4.

123. Ibid., Introduction, p. 3.

129. Ibid., p. 75.

130. Ibid., pp. 142–43.

131. Ibid., p. 193.

61

132. E. g., *kāṭho kandhane: kāṭho* is a stray dog or sponger; *kandhane* refers to someone who wears the *kandhani* or loin-cloth belt—both terms are traditional insults directed at Brahmans.

133. *Pramithas,* p. 174.

134. Ibid., p. 67. See, e.g., Joshi, *Mahākavi Devkoṭā ra Unkā Mahākāvya,* p. 286.

135. *Pramithas,* pp. 48–49.

136. Joshi, *Mahākavi Devkoṭā ra Unkā Mahākāvya,* pp. 261–62.

137. L. P. Devkota, *Sunko Bihāna* (Kathmandu: Sajha Prakashan, 1961), p. 18.

138. Ibid., p. 19.

139. Quoted in N. Pande, *Mahākavi Devkoṭā,* pp. 197–98. The last poems in English, on the other hand, strike a Western reader as formal, rhetorical, and, in terms of diction, early nineteenth-century and occasionally unidiomatic.

Selected Poems

Dreams of Nature and Nepal

Spring

What a season's here!
rainbowing the earth,
driving hares mad,
bees buzzing and the birds restless,
lightning in the sinews
and commotion in the heart.

So it was
in creation's primeval dawning,
in the waves' first heaving,
when the first lamps were lit;

the moment when
Shiva opens his closed lids
and Gauri's blush reddens the Himalayan peaks;*

or when
the lump of Vikram's heart
stirred
at the first glimpse of Urvashi,†
the sun at a standstill—
look now!
—like a wound above the sunset peaks.

A butterfly dances
(soul of a liberated sage),
taking this earth rich in honey
for heaven.

*Gauri, spouse of Shiva, is known by many names, including Parvati, the
daughter of the mountains.

†The love of Vikram (Pururavas) for the nymph Urvashi is celebrated in one of
Kalidasa's dramas.

The titillated dove
speaks what's in its heart—
saffron-love for the whole world.

We have all gone through the white gates
of branches hung with plum blossoms,
we have sat with fairies in the story-world
where buds can speak.

The air is stirring,
heavy with scattered fragrance.
Bunched-up hearts are itching to let go
and fling out sweet-scented worlds.

publ. 1956*

*The date at the end of each poem indicates the year of composition unless
preceded by "publ.," in which case, the year of composition being uncertain,
the date of first publication is given instead.

68

Clearing Morning in the Month of Magh*

How the sky has cleared this morning!
the blueness spreading like a netted veil.
So Valmiki's heart, like this sky, was cleansed
when Rama's dawning came.
The heavens speckle briefly with the crane's blood
and the compassionate verse
comes as a wave, a breath of that sky.
The bird regards this dawning as a festival;
the day-wandering sun is rising,
burning away to gold as it flies.
Toward the human future a finger points
from a tree's hand—an era quivering in the East.
Day speaks in a little voice—listen with care:
the web of the heart resounds.
Brahma, who envisioned all creation,
forms to an eastern diamond, turns dark
and disappears.
A clear flock of cranes floats in brightness,
stirring the tender wing of joy to life's rhythm.
On the tree-top the ray like a bird
came first to settle,
sang a music of secret rainbows
and slipped away.
With a whir the bird inside me
begins to move its wings.

1956

*Magh corresponds to late January and early February. Valmiki, reputed author of the *Rāmāyaṇa,* first spoke in metrical verse (and thus discovered the art of poetry) when moved to compassion by the sight of a crane killed by a hunter. Brahma is the god who created the universe. He may originally have been a solar deity and in some myths is born of the ether.

Beans and Rice and Mustard Greens*

We used to tramp along
on that long road of sorrow
seething with pain
tap tap tapping,
every moment seeing thousands
like ourselves
tracking down a sound of common hope
from the human heart
of which the soul is a little gulp of emotion,
tramping on the path
tap tap tapping.

The doctors listen to the human heart
through their stethoscopes
and extract a romantic meaning—
they say they hear "love-dove love-dove,"
and spread the lie far and wide,
as though some lovesick pigeon had made his nest
in a flock of dreams and said,
Oh Brother!
and sang the dreams of Shirin and Farhad.†
But I am compelled to say
that medical science is telling lies
with that sentimental meaning.

*"Dāl-bhāt-ḍuku," literally, lentils, cooked rice, mustard greens, a common
meal in the Kathmandu Valley, especially among poorer Nepalis. Because of
the rhyme of "ḍuku" and "cuckoo" and the onamatopoeic suggestion of the
heartbeat the translator was tempted to keep the Nepali phrase. In the Indian
poetic tradition the cuckoo is associated with spring and the awakening of
love. In the original poem "love-dove" and many other words are in English.

† Famous star-crossed Persian lovers.

And in the present realistic age
why should I blush to say it?
Feeling out the heart,
pondering and reckoning,
crystallizing the objective idea,
I found some other cuckoo saying
"Beans and rice and mustard greens!"

In the inner soul's vast forest
the bird-twitter of all human hearts
says this much in its true voice—
that without which all honor's lost
and one simply dies,
the beating of the universal heart
echoes
"Beans and rice and mustard greens!"

Concealed with coat and vest,
hidden deep in the heart,
it boasts a superficial glory,
the heartbeat dies to say it—
still, why should I be ashamed?
Take it hot or take it tender,
what does the plain-speaking poet fear?
This first tremor of the soul,
idyllic luxuriant creation,
with a hero for every mood,
a-tremble with feeling, singing of desire,
deity presiding over all the arts:
duk-duku duk-duku duk-duku,
beans and rice and mustard greens!

Stuck together in the flesh,
fastened up with the heart,
the living marrow undiminished—
eternal echo under the breast,
numbering every breath,

it tells it tells it tells it true,
cuckoo of the gross material body:*
"Beans and rice and mustard greens!"

In the primal waters
in the first throb of Vishnu's navel†
this host of greens was born.
On their way to the kitchen these beans
have been converted to divine energy;
as the philosophical voice came into them
they assumed a domestic garb.
It's rice that makes the whole world
proclaim the millstone's song
all along the path,
everyone husking rice,
frantic or exhausted,
and the echoes all agree—
cuckoo of the gross material body!
"Beans and rice and mustard greens!"

Oh gentlemen take heed!
what is this hypocrisy?
In a quiet moment
while the clock ticked its artificial tick-tick-tick
lying on my bed I thought,
Isn't it all just beans
and rice and mustard greens?

Without it the storms would flare,
there'd be revolution,
there'd be devastation,
the earth would weep.

---

*Annamaya kośa—a stock phrase in the Upanishads for the human body
nourished with food.

†According to Vaishnava mythology Brahma, creator of the world, sprang
from Vishnu's navel.

What's the fundamental basis of civilization?
Why should I try in vain to hide it?
Beans and rice and mustard greens.

The man who doesn't grasp philosophy
is a deep basket full of pride,
boasting of his blindness.
Let the understanding understand
what they fight and die for
and do all their laboring for,
nationalization the penance only for today,
the problem of the age.
Can the ship of state proceed
with these dumb sheep to lead it?

Look! Once at Aryaghat,*
at the royal throne of God,
on the stone bed,
the search hopeless,
and the world's morality shot,
a man says at the end,
opening his mouth to die,
"Oh Lord of Heaven, don't be harsh!
Be merciful.
I didn't get them on earth
and didn't look anywhere else,
thinking they would be in heaven.
Uh uh! Lord! Uh uh, Lord—
Beans and rice and mustard greens
Beans and rice and mustard greens!"

publ. 1956

---

* At Pashupatinath, where people are taken to die, often lying on stone slabs
with their feet in the river.

73

Unknown

The speaker is perhaps a woman of Kathmandu whose husband has gone to Lhasa to trade (a so-called *sotālā*) and lingered on there, taking a Tibetan wife. This situation provides the subject matter for Dor Bahadur Bista's interesting (and still untranslated) novel *Sotālā* (1976).

In Lhasa there must be musk deer,
    there must be gold in Lhasa.
There must be magic in Lhasa's river
    and moonlight burning the peaks.

There must be grand temples in Lhasa,
    in Lhasa the long robes.
I've never gone but my longing to go
    sees the land of gold.

Beyond the clouds, past the sunshine
    of Gosainthan, is Lhasa.
Unknown, the sweet mouth-harp's twang
    and, oh! the talk of the nightingales.

In Lhasa there's the living Buddha
    and the chilly days.
Beyond the reach of eyesight
    my heart imagining leaps high
to see the golden fleece.

Someone tell that Lhasa man
    beside the Turquoise River,
like a bird in a cage a girl
    weeps and longs to catch hold
of the hem of his robe.

Alas! I won't reach Lhasa in this lifetime,
    the roads will wash away,
I won't see the unknown, won't understand
    the talk of the nightingales,
alas, the talk of the nightingales.

publ. 1967

Cascades

From the summit of the hills
  I watched the waters fall.
In my heart the lamps lit up
  and twinkled by the thousands.
In the water of that cascade
  how great the hidden power!
How many electric lights
  one could see burning in it.
But alas thus scattered
  the water flows in vain,
and we ignore the secret gifts
  that dwell inside it.
On the mountain peaks
  of all our human hearts
are there not just such cascades
  of clean free-flowing waters?
If only there were inside us
  lovely cascades by the thousands—
oh but the pity of it!
  the world is still dark.

publ. 1953

Morning Song

Rise up, beloved,
the day has come,
the morning rose is blooming.
Happy dreams
spread in the sky,
the force falls on the lotus.

The bright-clad robin*
sings his plaint,
leaves and branches waken.
Lazily the first
frost-drops quiver,
the night explodes in atoms.

Now the golden ray
has kissed the peaks
and woken the gilded temple spires.
Now the first star
takes her leave—
oh lover, the dawn is going.

Drops of water
glisten and tremble,
the river flings off the mist.
A chilly wind
will come to tease
the sleepy-natured bud.

*The magpie-robin, known as "dhobi" or "dhobini" (washerman, washer-woman), known for its sweet singing in springtime in the Kathmandu Valley.

The dream is opening
the eastern sky,
the daylight clears and sharpens.
Now shapes and colors
are opening, dearest,
and bells are ringing Heaven.

Forget the embrace
of darling darkness,
the rays are thrusting down.
The first drop of dew
glitters and says,
"Awaken, beloved, my flower treasure!"*

Sunshine has struck
all the drowsy world,
Nature sets herself to glisten.
Now stir the sleeping
leaves of the spirit,
let the skies inside your pupils shine.

Wings now have flown
to golden lands
to see them rising, beautiful.
When the eastern wind
has roused you,
will you not open your tight-shut eyes?
Oh waken now, my lord,
and call!

publ. 1969

---

*Phūl-dhan: a term for the beloved, but in this context I have chosen to
translate it literally.

Rainbow

Melting treasure of creation,
O Shravan* rich in colors!
suspend arching above the peaks
the radiant rainbow
of your art.
Ray-woven in the flow of mists
new archer's bow
shooting its flower shafts
into the heart of the eye,
vibrant with new emotions.

The first poet,
then drops of water from the eyes—
rays rose, rays fell,
reached Heaven
to touch the earth.

Did truth ever before
fuse in such crazy hues?
Did the lashes of the Creation sprite
spill such sparkle,
applying first
collyrium—
mingling a new bride's joy and woe
glistening in the fringe?

Is this the river
of the seven tones unheard?
the gorgeous marriage
of loving sunlight and shadow?

*The Nepali month corresponding to July–August.

cataract of colors
or showers of grief and pleasure,
of murmured sounds?

A magic bird, water its body,
swaying like a flower,
bridge linking peak to peak—
why has it shone forth,
this heavenly spectacle?
The delicate nightingales are singing,
hurrah! in vision and in sound
supreme triumph of art.

Tell me, why are you shining?
would you join together
riven heaven and earth
or sundered god and man?

Witch light of splintered rays,
deep-hued prism!
Dense particles of water
all turn to butterflies,
to burn their ecstasy.

Self-sacrificer,
teach the cloud
to die!
Teach the earth
to thrill,
O rainbow!*

1956

* There are at least three different versions of this poem in print, of which the
shortest is translated here. Devkota himself translated a slightly longer version
of the poem. In most printings the final word is not *indreni* (rainbow) but
Indrāni, the spouse of the god Indra, but *indreni* is clearly intended and the
poet himself concludes his translation with "You the Rainbow!"

Minpachas

This is the name for a period of fifty days in midwinter when the weather in the Kathmandu Valley is at its coldest.

Minpachas has come!
Water longs to turn to glass
and even fish seek shelter.
People hanker for the bright days
but the sun's gone too far south—
how thin the sunshine now!
Shadows fall, and it's the time
of weeping Nature's desolation.

That sprite called Emerald takes
all green foliage to her parents' house.
Her girl friends are calling her—
but she won't be back for half a year.
How empty the world down here!
Even the birds are sad, and the earth's limbs
have gone slack,
as though its youth had flown.

Our shortened day has little time
to wander the path of light;
it loves the sunshine of the distant Polestar,
ever covering the South,
that smiles for six months
in the sun's embrace.
The North descends today,
in tears, casting off all adornment.

Because day's sparkling jewel
sets in the South
shadowed Nature cries out,
Don't forget me!
Cold blows the wind, sorrow's sigh
for vanished treasure.
We very rich are poor now,
our happiness gone gray.

As though the year had aged,
hair and beards are frosted.
The waters are like energy dried up,
and still they sparkle.
Withered leaves are all a-shudder,
and dried sticks are everywhere
looking like pale
hunchbacked women on the move.

The woods have lost their charm,
marked with the fog and rime.
Just like our bodies
the shrubs turn all to thorn.
Fingernails go blue and throb,
the snow's bite hurts.
Shivering and trembling the heart
and life itself are struck with fright.

The cold is like the touch of death.
The warm is life.
The world's love now is for the fire,
and there's no riches like shining flame.
The blaze roars cheerily
like friendly scrapping children,
happily dancing as the essence
of the heat mounts, beautiful.

But firewood is scarce and dear
and quickly turns to ashes.
The more we try to drive away the cold
the colder it will get.
If you haven't money for woolens
how your bones will chatter:
the life of the people of Nepal—
that's all it is!
But the dreams were beautiful.

publ. 1964

To a Dark Cloudy Night

O light-engulfing
dense black nightfall,
the day's unfeeling corpse,
igniting the sunset peaks
with treasures of many shapes and colors,
like some ascetic woman
of the cremation ground,
thick tangled tresses in wild disorder,
smeared with the universal ash,
motionless, entranced:
have you entered into ecstasy
and vanished on the snowy ridges?—
vast death's shadow,
form taken by the immense void.

Like an ocean all solid blackness,
clashing planes of terrifying shades
surging from earth to sky,
every instant   every instant
you smash the reefs of our consciousness
and frighten earth's poor children.

Great sleep
descending on unmoving feet,
shutting in the earth,
light's negation from the underworld—
before the horror of you
living souls must close their eyes
and swoon away.

This much only is it then,
all the dazzling, varied history of the world?

Heart of a mute mystery invisible,
Speak, breathless darkness!
Do unheard tides of the great emptiness,
flooding black, exploding and engulfing,
batter and devour the shores?—
Is this life like a vessel
filled only with
the void?

O earth, O earth!
I shrivel to a mustard seed,
pulverized,
my head blanked out utterly.

Doubting my own existence
that glimmers, minute particle of brightness,
like that paltry star
in the fissure of a cloud,
suffocated,
minuscule,
without a hope.

You robber of all my vanished wealth,
black prison of things past,
split, burst out,
break open your own ruthless breast,
female beautiful as the world's cremation!
Lo, mindless night,
within you is the Imperishable,
the Imperishable
the stars   the stars!

1956

Dawn

The night was a corpse,
darkness falling
   like ink;
coming down in every
shape and color
   the frost.

The awful faintness fading,
the morning breeze begins
   to blow.
A chilly tickling
pain begun in dreams
   uncaused.

The eastern light
went foggy yellow
   like smoke.
Rising at dawn, pearls
sparkled in the sky,
   turned gray.

In a red of rhododendrons
the goddess of the dawn
   looks down.
Sweet-throated roosters
she rouses up
   to crow.

Conchs are blown, bells
ring out the morning
   music.

The sunken world
swims up again, youthful in
    the light.

All the flowers and weeds
put on the dazzle
    of pearls.
The wind grows stronger
and shakes the priceless
    splendor.

Like a new dream over
the eastern chaos burned
    the gold.
Uncaused it flared up,
blazing, melting, the good
    bright fire.

Creating with golden brush
the painter day
    came forth.
Lamps lit up on the peaks,
for one instant powerful
    magic.

River mists draw away,
towers glitter, their gold
    melting.
Dewy with the nine colors
on its stem the lotus
    flickers.

Supple and luminous,
aureate, carmine,
    rosy,

the new day spreads
with the downy richness
   of birds.

All those sparkling ponds, oh,
turn into lovely
   Lhasas.
Baby birds, mouths open, oh,
are stirring, ready to take
   the plunge.

Rising again the world
finds new labor for
   the morning.
and brings back the nectar,
splashing colors on
   the morning.

Hope rises new
with news of the new
   morning,
demanding that everyone
make an investment
   in fate.*

publ. 1968

*Karamko lagān: a difficult image to compress; "lagān" is money invested for profit and "karam" is a colloquial variant of "karma," a word that is as rich in denotation as in connotation—action, works, accumulated merit and debt from earlier lives, fate.

Private Visions

Birthday

I have diminished like a waterclock
dripping twenty-five drops like pearls;

    twenty-five birds who've set out singing
    joy and sorrow as they cruise the skies.

I have moved ahead twenty-five steps
closer to the funeral pyre.

    The joy of a birthday!
    Only this time I wept.

Remembering all the lovely years
I shed my tears in silence.

    Twenty-five winters and twenty-five springs:
    the first delicious honey of life.

What's left now is the dregs,
burdens, worries, a savorless life.

    Enticing pictures, the colors faded,
    tired, shuffling in the sunlight.

Twenty-five rounds the earth danced,
progress gained twenty-five steps:

    hero climbing the steep slope
    moved up twenty-five hard degrees.

True and noble laboring has reaped
many a golden harvest.

    Oh the drum of my heart is taking me
    steadily toward the pyre.

While I sit around and fidget,
Rise up, rise up! says the heart's king.

   The sun lord of the world
   came dreaming near the sunset.

Your message I have quite forgotten—
for just an instant flash a hint!

   I lost my human body like a beast,
   the light was in my heart.

A fog came covering up that lamp;
I trembled then and wept.

   Either waken or put out
   the light of my existence.

Give me a heart that can weep
   wise bodhisattva!
Decorate this winter
   with sprouting leaves.

   Give news of a new awakening:
   the salvation of one fallen.

1934

Pipedreams

The original title, *Bhūt Savār,* means haunted or obsessed, but in the colloquial speech of Kathmandu it suggests delusion or pipedreams.

Conquering Alexander had
a tiger's whiskers,
and what a sword in his hand!
and what fists—
worth millions!

He sat and sulked, sulked—
a whim.
Did something get away?
Everybody licking and licking and
getting fat—
what a shock
for the conqueror of the world.

"What does he want?"
He says:
"Ha ha ha ha—don't block the sunlight."
Behold the power of wisdom
over mere weaponry.

How wonderful the charity of the bankrupt!
The free heart's worshipper
laughs, in my heart the wretch
laughs, rejects and curses
the hoarded wealth and plunder
and kicks them away.

1956

Friday Night Eleven O'Clock

It's eleven o'clock this Friday night—
thank God! the good deliverance,
this my little Nirvana,
companion for an hour,
everybody sleeping:
this is my good day.

Heart reaches the other world,
eternal, joyful.
Let me open the window:
private realm of Nature the queen.
The breeze, ambrosial sigh,
restores the earth to life;
a breath of wetness
from the leaves of drenched forests faraway:
the shaper of the moving clouds,
free guest and fair, a sinewy wanderer,
flies up as before,
stirring the inmost soul,
most light and graceful gandharva.*
Come honored guest invisible,
recount the moon's romance,
how the lover was entangled
in the net of the monsoon—
come wind, tell the story,
tender, tender and good.

* In Indian mythology a celestial musician.

94

Misty the East, misty, blue twilit fog,
the South a white, white cave,
the West deep blue.
You called to Nature,
summoned her all day long.
Now nothing can be seen,
nothing can be heard until
breaking the blind circle
I hear just barely, just barely see,
the heart full of silent speech;
in this good moment I hear
a thousand nights.

I remember, twice we poured the water jug.
Toward evening the smiling lightning
burst and tore the veil,
and was afflicted, seeing the poet
dead, victim of fierce fever—
was it fear or wearing away?
I found just barely, just barely came:
come, give your vision.
Of many kinds are your
dances of desire
worthy of worship.

Mist over the fields far to the southeast,
as though the earth spirit had breathed
on the mirror of the moon,
tossing the yellow tufts of wheat,
thirsting for the green, as though to say
Let me adorn myself;
lazy the wave of its own conceiving,
lo, earth spirit sniffs the scent of jasmine,
and all the heaven spirits settle
spinning and spinning cotton.

I say thanks, thanks to the one
who keeps me in a house like this.
All bad luck dies today: I drink
nectar and I weep;
the fever of the whole week
disappears, well-being has no limit.
In this vastness someone laughs
and gathers foam flowers
far on the other side.
See, in my mind—
pliant vine of flickering dreams—
the lamp of highest bliss
blazes in the snow.

So many brightly colored pictures
alive on the cloudy red-silk-cotton tree!
Let them wither and fade.
Language dwells in water,
every moment change
and movement and growth.
Shall I not remember? The poet's heart
surely performs its labor
in its own privacy.

For one hour I talked
silently
in some communion.
I opened the window of an enormous house
inside the heart.
I moved with spread wings
over waves of nectar,
found freedom in flight, swung in moondust.
So rich am I, Mother! On earth I find heaven,
my forty-seven poor years
jewels today.

"Praise," says Nature the queen,
"praise be to you!"
Better to live a few full moments
than a long life unfulfilled.

1956

Quatrain

Oh had I been some green and lovely vine
I would have sucked ambrosia and put out fine
  flowers;
glad-hearted song birds would have come to carol—
well, my country's turned ambrosial but this poetry's
  barbarous.

1958

The Season of Life

While it's still the season of life
    plow, plow the field
        of the heart.
Do not lie barren while the rain
    pours down the pure white water
        of the mind.
From the infinite ocean
    the monsoon has come
        drifting in.
The heart's soil bursts with flowers,
    the song of the rains
        resounds.
Scorn the body—the cattle of the senses—
    buckle down and plow,
        plow the field.
Plant the seeds of karma in the world
    by the thousands, and bring
        the rich lush fields to bear.
While it's the season of life
    plow it and plant it
        and make it bloom.
Cruel time, alas, returns
    to no one: and so, don't
        lie sleeping.
Plant, plant all these seeds right now
    so the grain may ripen
        afterward.
And later when harsh winter
    comes to you
        don't cry.

publ. 1953

Memory

When clouds drift over the earth,
  over life a sorrow,
when the tears rain down
  on parched despairing hearts,
when lament is everywhere
  recollecting the heart's pain
remember then the full-moon nights
  in dream cities after the earthquake.

In the desert of vexation,
hand at your forehead,
existence becomes a curse,
success beyond the sandy wastes.
Within the alien, cruel jungle
of the world I call
when life's become a burden,
a tumult of the spirit,
in that same moment I remember
you, and the tears stop.

In memory the garden blooms,
  winning sap and color;
the sand turns fresh and green
  and cool waters play.
The cuckoo sings, quickening
  a tender spring in the heart.
The sandal-breeze begins to flow,
  full of your fragrant breath,
and in my memory rise from sleep
  the sweet sounds of your voice.

publ. 1935

Clay Lamp*

This little clay lamp
is stained all over black,
in the open world naive and good,
in silence bearing the flame
in which it has its pride.
Just pain is its adornment,
pain is its worldly joy.
Just to burn is its life,
       heat its penance.

Flame burning and gathering
       says life is a little clay cup,
              life is pain,
to burn—the essence of awareness,
       the idea—a thread of atoms and ashes,
              blood itself the fuel.

For whom are you blazing, flame?
       who garners the substance,
              this bird's beak pain,
                     tender moment of the pen?

Last night it rained
       and the rain said,
the fire garlands the intellect,
       some unknown universal poet
              writes on the page
                     the freshness of the age.

*Written with the title "Vednā Sphoṭ" (A Burst of Pain); the Banaras publishers indicate the change of title but give no explanation.

Like you the lamp is burning.
    My tavern is serenity,
        the flame my girl who brings the wine;
As with a beak of bitter fate
    it writes the poem,
        the garland for the heart.

Only flame, only flame
    must be the substance
        of pain.

publ. 1967

Echoes

Confused murmur of the sonorous heart,
rilling waters of the full spirit,
  pacified, in the dark, apart;

air throbbing within the flute,
gentle tremor responding to the player,
  flowing in the Jumna like time;*

words fly and strike the sitar,
strings sound back in answer—
  strange touch and strange effect!

What slumbering vibration
can the world contrive to strike
so it will echo back
  in harmony?

publ. 1958

* A reference to Krishna as flute player in Vrindavan on the banks of the
sacred Yamuna (Jumna).

Songs of the Gaine

The poems in this section are taken from the posthumously published collection entitled *Gāine Gīt,* the songs of the Gaine. The Gaine (pronounced approximately guy-nay) are a community of wandering minstrels who traditionally play a variety of *sārangī,* a kind of violin, and improvise songs, often of a devotional nature. Devkota's variations on Gaine themes are mystical, fanciful, and frequently obscure, with sometimes baffling syntax, and in the original manuscript, they are occasionally indecipherable. But they make a beguiling collection and, apart from their poetic interest, are significant as representing Devkota's chief essays in *bhakti* poetry, the great tradition of Indian devotional song which reached its zenith in the fifteenth and sixteenth centuries and has never completely died out.

The Gaine

Spilling oceans and tearing my breast
I've come from the hills
singing songs of a moment
with my three-stringed fiddle.*

I made friends with the waves
and discovered their rhythms.
From the ear into the heart
today I've brought a nest.

I bring the magic of the gone-before,
I am the daughter of today.
I bring tidings of the after-time,
my eyes a burning flame.

Sweet fiddle scraping
that dwells in all,
the sleeper in the strings
I waken with my singing.

I wander from yard to yard—
a little colored bird—
always asking for
a handful of rice like pearls.

Child youth and old man sway
to my simple singing
and bring a few handfuls
of grain like tears.

*Sārangī.

To Go On Singing

Why do I want to go on singing
in sunlight and shadow?
To keep on flowing and not stop talking
and making pictures?

I want to write like the clouds
in Rani Pokhri;*
I want to make the flowers bloom
and carve them into tenderness.

Come now, tell me! the murmur
of flowing sonorous water.
I dream of heaven and I want
to pull it down.

This is merely longing's flood
trying to flow away.
Ever worshipping the sea
the water turns to cloud.

Seeking the world within the sea
wind-climbing waters!
This is merely the fruit
of the Lord's impatience.

Strength of the sea trying
to be little waves.

*The "Queen's Pool" in Kathmandu. See note on "A Ballad of Rani Pokhri,"
p. 127.

Foggy Morning

Today I'm inside the fog,
but still at dawn that light
of glistening worlds
has suddenly broken through.

Flowering golden he dwells
in a fragrant land,
all well in his aloneness
on the tip of the ray.

We cannot see our path,
we heave cold sighs.
Hope turns into a bird
and life sinks in the dawning gray.

Nature's cloud descends,
spreading form and color.
The Lord's illusions come
with the magic of what's-not-clear.

Seeing in the dawn is
remembering separation.
In the ray's threads the cloud,
creation on a loom of shadows.

Little bird who lives in the cloud
sang a pleasing song and sought the Lord
in the sweet shadows of
illusion's forest.

Gold the cloud of joy and grief;
enlisting all the stars, Lord,
you wrapped this heavy world
in a net.

Dwelling in the world—
mixed milk and water—
heavenly geese discriminate
and drink the buttermilk.*

With breast and womb of stone
the dawn put out its flowers;
we have the power to pluck
and touch and smell.

In the clarity of our eyes
clouded over blind,
Krishna with a magic spell
spread out the fog.

Inside the cloud I saw
lines of golden threads.
I pluck the foggy flowers and offer
pictures to the Lord.

Varieties of the Infinite
like love · · · · †
A cloud bird he made
my soul · · · ·

Sweet Krishna in the dawn
in the web of illusion.
· ·

· · · · · · · · · · · · · · · · · · · ·

Hamsa, geese, traditionally have the power to extract soma or milk from
mixed milk and water. In the Upanishads the term often is a symbol of the
soul, and in modern colloquial Nepali the expression "the hamsa has flown"
is a euphemism for dying.

† In the published version of the *Gāine Gīt* the Nepali editors used this symbol
to indicate illegible words in the manuscript.

The ray came with the compassion
of water from the sea,
into the foggy wood's enchantment
brought tenderness.

Shadow sweeter than seeing,
glimpse better than perception;
into the waking eye
the dream flickering.

On earth better than in heaven
the sweetness of the fog—
love's shadows you have cast, Lord,
here and there.

I found the black thirst,
the magic of this search;
and within the pain of not-having
a thousand tender blessings.

Sweet forest shadows of
imaginings, imagination.
Tell me, with what kind of love,
Lord, do you half-hide yourself?

Close by and without tears
· · · · · · · · · · · · they look,
like me they fill their eyes
with daybreak's common sense.

In mortality's darkness
the cup of nectar.

I Said (1)

I said, Well then, do I
have so very little?
—always hungry and
sobbing through my fiddle.

He said, But hunger *is*
all the flavor I have.*
I'm in the clutches of
the one who makes me cry.

I said, Well then, do I
have so very little?
—hope always flying off
on its crippled wings.

He said, Greater than flying
the confines of the nest.
In a twinkling the lightning
blows away reality—
praise be to the cycle
of birth and birth again.

I said, Well then, do I
have so very little?
I will do and *I* will get,
then I'll throw away these rags.

The answer came: the sandal paste,
rubbed away to nothing, found itself.
In "me" alone there's no being
but in the eyes of you and me meeting.

Ras, which means not only flavor or taste but esthetic sentiment, essential emotion, etc.

cloud water water cloud
if I am merely to be blotted out—
how much has entered into me!
dying for you, blotted out.

With hope I've come to make an offering.
You say to me, Blot out God—
come into me, *I* am the offering,
futile all this weeping.

I said, Well then, Sir,
have I so very little?
All the "mine" has gone empty,
and my plate is bare.

He said, So long as one
grain is left over
my full essential form cannot
fit snug into the heart.
Picking and choosing while all is empty
I climb atop emptiness,
take light for my vehicle
and come learning you.

Oh what a fool I used to be!
A great king was I then,
but I sold away the ruling
of the world—and walked
to beg for a fistful of dust.
I begged in my own house,
staring at my own door.
The Supreme Lord made me laugh
and called me into the dark.

I Said (2)

I said, I can't, you know!
   He joined his hands together.
Burden of the world, I said.
   His tears flowed.

Make no request of me,
   he said, alas.
At the foot of my throne
   the world will finally tremble.

I said, No, oh no!
   He said, Sir!
The debt of pain you bear
   is the peak of your greatness.

What business is it of yours? I said
   and much vexed, turned away.
Tear shining in the infinite,
   life throbbing inside death.

Fire kindling in the ashes,
   he said, Abandoning you,
the world, still vexed, has lost
   the universe-sustaining answer.

I said then, turning, What
   can I expect to get?
He said, Just see
   the life-throb of the Infinite.

But why for me destruction
   and the torment of creation?
Your bliss is for another life
   the land called heaven.

He Said

No no! he said,
    only a subtle wind.
Hope inside the breaking heart
    budded to a sound.

My feet turned trembly,
    the road was crooked.
I understood
    the more I climbed the weaker I got.

I said, I'm staying here.
    just give me this rock.
The snow fell all the more
and loneliness told the story:
    there's no ending here.

The more I climbed the fewer the trees,
    just bare stumps.
In doubt and growing weary—
    alas, one must accept it.

Ready I was to die
    when I reached the shining peak.
Again I stopped; my heart beat—
    I grasped the impulse to live.

No no! he said,
    set your foot
at the final twist
    of the cord of life;

climb till you die
    your heart bursting at last,
after you've looked and taken
    the measurement of the height.

A Thousand Deaths   A Thousand Lives

How I used to like to dance, Sir,
in the green wood of Vrindavan.*
How I used to like to chatter, Lord,
as though I were a wild bird.

In the jungle I'm all alone,
the earth in darkness.
The cold storm rages,
and no one to cry pity.

A thousand times I became a corpse,
a thousand times awakened.
The knot of life keeps coming undone:
within, memory full of hope
takes on a thousand lives.

With the hope that you're not cruel
I'll come into the dark.
There I'll stop and set my heart
to dance for you.

* Vrindavan is the name of the forest by the Jumna River, in northern India,
associated with Krishna's childhood and youth, held sacred by his devotees.

Sweeper

In our hands the workbroom,
the dust of the road.
Inside, our lovely truths
keep opening and opening.

Age after age we wept
tears of servitude.
We offered up our souls,
scorning the flesh.

Pledged to the fierce bed
of arrows, oath of the poor,
in the ecstasy of enduring
we're immersed in God.

We made labor our friend
and searched in the darkness.
We chose that God who says,
In the darkness I become a lamp.

Believing human feet are clean—
such is our dharma.
God kissed our hands and laughed.
To serve is our destiny.

Our Lord is the friend of the poor
with hands to wipe our tears.
Love is our holy essence,
Disgrace our fall.

I've Had It

I've had it, Lord! Don't come
to the house of darkness.
Rather grant my wish:
destroy memory. Why make me shed
so many useless tears?

I'm a corpse, the night would say.
You made the teardrops shine
and opened up page after page
of anguish and desire, made me weep
songs unheard, like dreams.

Had I but been content
that there is nothing
I'd have shut up and slept.
Had there been the sound of a footfall
I'd have pricked up my ears.
You lied with that "There's nothing,"
and made me cry in my sleep.

But if my dreams don't sleep
what grief is that to me?*

*Keko pīr malāī? The expression may just as well mean "what kind of grief
(i.e., how great) is my grief!"

Public Views

Sleeping Coolie

On his back a fifty-pound load,
spine bent double,
six miles straight up in the January snow,
naked bones,
two rupees worth of life in his body
to challenge the mountain.

Cloth cap black with sweat
and worn to shreds,
body swarming with lice and fleas,
mind dulled.
It's like sulphur, but how tough
this human frame!

The bird of his heart panting,
sweat and breath.
On the cliff his hut, kids trembling:
hungry griefs!
No greens to eat; his wife combs the woods
for weeds and nettles.

Beneath the snow peak
of this more than human hero's mountain,
conquering nature, with a hoard of pearls—
the sweat on his forehead—
and above only the lid of night
bright with stars:
in this night he is rich with sleep.

1958

The Beggar

See there! a beggar's come. He totters,
   lifts up pathetic eyes—
the silent light of misery—
   and plays the thin string of hope
in the bright sunshine of the yard.
   With one round tear he gives
   the history of his life.

Look, look at those rags and tatters!
   Alas, unpitying time.
Feeble and ailing on the road of life
   he trembles, he shivers;
hand unsteady, fearful, the forlorn fellow
   holds out his threadbare bag.

Behold the frost of years
   fallen on his head;
see the hollows in his face
   deepened by streams of tears,
and the deep scars on his chest—
   erosion of the passing days.

Panting and shaking he stands
   held up by a lifeless stick
and pours out his silent lament,
   his heart's cry bursting out,
the voice tearing your own heart:
   "One handful of rice!"
The single claim of a whole lifetime—
   "One handful of rice."

The weeping of the inmost heart
　　of a man before men,
this begging from his brothers
　　for a handful of compassion.
In the yard bright with sunshine
　　what a gloomy sight!
—the sorrowing of the fern
　　amid the laughter of roses.

Who can he be, whose child?
　　whose father so unlucky?
What mother's eyes burned like two lamps
　　when she took him to her breast?
What was the hope that opened up his eyes
　　to the eyes of sun and moon?
Why has the lamp of his life
　　grown dim and faded away?

This same beggar man once stood
　　before Lord Buddha's gaze,
the same figure, the same voice
　　crying out the heart's anguish.
Through him the sea of great compassion
　　sent the echoes of its waves;
in such a guise he humbled the pride
　　of Bali and made it pure.*

Fallen from black clouds
　　to enter into darkness
is he God or is he a beggar?

* As a dwarf in his fifth avatar, Vishnu claimed from Bali, lord of the three
worlds, all he could cover in three strides, and covered all three worlds—the
earth with one, heaven with another, and the atmosphere with the third—
thus reclaiming them for the gods.

He speaks—God inside the heart—
and wanders, house to house, yard to yard,
　　speaks with the voice of pain,
his heart drenched with pity.

Distilling tears that never end,
　　flowing through all the ages,
opening the eternal lips,
　　God speaks from the grieving heart.
He comes upon this earth
　　asking pity from his brothers;
he begs for alms—God himself,
　　a beggar in my yard.

publ. 1940

Pilgrim

What temple are you going to, pilgrim,
  what temple are you going to?
What ritual objects will you use
  and how will you take them with you?
Riding on men's shoulders, what
  celestial city will you enter?
Of bones the lovely pillars,
  of solid flesh the walls!
this golden roof made of the brain,
  of the senses all the doors,
the veins—waves of coursing rivers
  and the temple the unbounded self.
What temple are you going to, Pilgrim,
  to the door of what temple?
On the fair throne of the spirit
  the earth's Lord ruling;
this golden light of the intellect
  the crown on his head,
this fair temple of the body—
  center of the universe.
Inside is God, outside the eyes—
  what town do you go looking for?
God dwells in the depths—
  how far you drift over the surface!
Are you seeking? Apply your heart
  flaring bright as a glowing lamp.
Your companion on the journey—God,
  walking with you, pilgrim.
God kisses the hand
  that does the golden work.

His secret fingers touch
   the brows of those who serve.
At the edge of the road God sings
   in the melodies of birds.
In songs of grief God sings
   humankind's afflictions.
But nowhere does he show himself
   to the fleshly eye of the blind.
What temple are you going to, pilgrim,
   to what strange new land?
Turn back, turn back! Oh go and catch
   the feet of humankind!
Rub balm on all the sorrow
   and on the smarting wounds.
As you are men, so you must make
   God's heavenly face to smile.

publ. 1941

A Ballad of Rani Pokhri*

"What's down there in the water, father?
  Is anyone living down there, father?"
    "The king's palace and the great men's houses
    and all the court are deep down under."

"But where is the king?" "He's stone today."
  "Did he have a beautiful daughter?"
    "She's the golden fish who lurks and gleams
    and takes the crumbs we throw her."

"But why this fence?" "They say a beggar
came begging some food for his child.
  But they set the dog on him, and the king
  never woke up or saw a thing."

"Where is the king's sky-colored chamber?"
  "It's the green moss in the middle of the pool."
    "But what does the king eat?" "Water through all the
    ages,
    and only the weeds bow down before him."

publ. 1967

*Rani Pokhri, the "Queen's Pool," is a large, fenced-in pool in Kathmandu
near the royal residence of Narayanhiti and various Rana palaces. Devkota
may well have had the Ranas in mind when he wrote this poem during the
years of exile in Banaras.

Ballad of the Fair Sweeper*

Most lovely the sweeper girl Chameli
  so sweet of face—
just like a flower in bloom—
  and her voice sweet to the ear.

At dawn's reddening she comes
  to sweep the yard, when Daybreak,
that goddess, moves her golden broom
  sweeping stains from the eastern sky.

Sitting in his window Sundar Prasad
  sang a song of love,
how love goes beyond this earth.
Chameli heard it; in her eyes
  the round tears gathered.

Sundar gave her a fragrant leaf;
  Chameli made a little cup.
His mother said, "She's just like a whore
  pretending to be respectable!

The millionaire Brahman's daughter
  is learned, they say she's beautiful."
Says Sundar, "I won't marry her!
  I'd just as soon be dead."

"Chameli, here's five hundred rupees,
  all my money for the year."
Five times Chameli took the five notes
  and the evening turned to daylight.

*Sweeper—*camār,* i.e., untouchable. Chameli *(cameli)* is a jasmine and the lover's name, Sundar, means beautiful.

128

"Come to me, my child,
    wearing fine and clean and proper clothes."
The next day the girl comes running—
    who can it be—a royal princess?

At dawn Chameli's there,
    come to sweep the courtyard.
"Oh girl, my girl! Fill two pitchers
    and set them by the door!"

A stick in his hand, a watch on his wrist,
    Sundar says, "Oh Mother!
From this morning on I'm just a sweeper,
    by the Lord, I've thrown away my caste."

"Oh son, oh son!" "Don't call me son,
    you Brahman lady, oh!
For Chameli I Sundar
    freely and for love
    am born anew, oh!"

                                    publ. 1967

Child of the Times

Weak, weepy, pigeon-breasted,
forsaken,
dumpy, sniveling, shallow friend—
thorns!
whiny throat of the cat
in winter.

This is not the gauge of our future
far away.
The angels have cursed the earth,
cursed it deep.
Two there are who afflict the Lord—
the bastards.*

I see bright colored pictures,
child!
ripened apples, bursting pomegranates
red!
But how can new golden waves
come?

So great as this the angels'
scorn?
this carelessness and this compulsion
mingled?

---

*Rāṇḍa—this obscure line may be a punning reference to the two chief Ranas who before the revolution, in Devkota's view, afflicted both God and the earth.

"We shall not come," they said—
for why would they
be caught again down here?
How should the beautiful fall
down among the ugly crowd?

publ. 1976

Toward Dasain

At the autumn festival known as Dasain it is customary to sacrifice goats and buffaloes. All the adjectives attributed to the goat in this poem, and *boko,* the word for goat itself, are also used pejoratively to designate men of a licentious and destructive nature; the Ranas may be indicated and "Dasain" may euphemistically indicate the coming revolution.

> This goat is eating
> special grass.
> In our homes we have
> a different grain,
> thorns, thorns!
> He's black, white is our color,
> through and through.
> What a fat, sex-driven beast it is,
> roving free.
> Dasain will come!
> he the sacrifice,
> for us a festival—
> how far off can it be?

> publ. 1959,
> written ca. 1948
> in exile in Banaras

Children

Two Children's Poems from Putalī (Butterfly)

1. Dreams

All kinds of dreams! tell me, my friend,
    do they come stealing into your heart?—
winged, light, and very sweet—
    too swift for the mind to seize.

Like sparrows on whirring wings from far,
    flocking and scattering on the breeze,
so swiftly they're out of sight
    they just bring sadness to the mind.

Most pleasing are they to the heart,
    like the very sweetness of our land,
too far and hidden in the leaves
    for you to catch them in your hand.

And bringing sadness to this heart, my friend,
    this spirit ever looking for a path.
They move the spirit among gardens, then
    out of sight—but our sighs will never end.

2. Remembering

When I remember in my heart
    my grand, enchanting country
and the wind ruffles my hair
    tears fill my eyes.
How much I might have done,
    what splendid dreams fulfilled!

The heart says with its tears
   what many-mouthed Shesh might say.*
Why is it, oh why, do we
   shed our good tears constantly?
How much there is to say!
   How much there is to tell!
I pray Lord Shiva may
   see it in my heart.

publ. 1952

*Śeṣa, the serpent with a thousand heads who supports Vishnu.

Wind Country

On a chariot of the gods
midst roaring winds
in a net of skies
    I go flying—don't know where—
    while lying on the grass.
    of the forest.
You can't see the wheels
move in the rustling leaves
and flowers.
    The chariot of the mind
    keeps climbing steadily
    in joy.
Somewhere there's a country
of winds where the dreams flicker
and flash;
    they blossom like clouds
    and spread out beds
    of roses.
Such is the country I go to
where I taste many
savory dishes
    and converse for days
    with the company of gods
    and nymphs.
Over the blue sea travels
the shining chariot
of my mind.
    Drawn on I see heaven
    smiling, and I step
    right in.

King Indra and all the girls
celestial, and the fine
golden houses—
    when I have seen them I come
    home to the grass, and I feel
    well again.
Our heaven's there
where all the dreams
are golden:
    our flight is here
    inside the mind
    with the winds.
The more you wander the wind country
the more you see beauty
with the heart;
    your vision cleansed and light
    opening in the heart you find
    sweet music.

publ. 1968

Remembering the Wheat

In this sometimes obscure poem, the poet, recalling his childhood, conceives of the young wheat shoots as a bride, returning every season to the *maiti*—her father's house.

Supple mind runs to meet the morning in the wheatfield;
dewdrops catch a shape, then vanish in the wind.
Glittering rainbows of July excite my wonder;
she teases with a smile, I sniff and track her in the wind.
As though to say, "It's time to take me home, child,"
at first the young shoots bend and plunge and tense;
she smiles and says, "I don't let the wind
touch my budding body," as it tickles her stems,
and each time the breeze sways her she shrinks and feels
   ashamed.
Let the river have a bank, let there be yellow, let the earth be
   high,
let the poet's mind be filled with pleasure!
She spreads the joy.
I wandered in town, distracted, and the scent is here,
where the young shoots sing restless songs in the tender
   sunlight.
We uncovered many adolescent loves· · · · I remember:
but after ten months there she'll remember me
and she'll come home this year.

publ. 1964

In Memory of Three Deceased Children

The second stanza refers to the poet's second daughter, who died in 1935 at the age of two months; the third stanza to his second son, Krishnaprasad, who died at eleven in 1947 during his father's absence in exile (the "plunge into the wave"); and the final stanza to Prakash, the eldest son, who died in 1952 at the age of seventeen.

Light showers drizzling down (why do my eyes mist over?),
every moment lightning flares, rips the clouds and my heart.

It's like a tattered cloud—but still,
    should one's heart be wet for it?
Death plucked my first blossom in the bud,
cut and devoured the first piece of my heart.
Infant promise, tearful eyes—
smooth and deft the frosty hand fell on her.

I saw the motherland and wept, plunged into the wave—
in the time of darkness a heaven like this in tears!
My second son hid my shoes in the niche on the stairs
and said, "Don't go, daddy," tried to stop me—
I scolded and fled into the net.
"Did father call me?" he said
and went to heaven, scorched with hunger.

The oldest boy—lotus from the mud—
his intellect a flame,
deeply wise and quiet in his ways:
barren ground, the sunshine brief and the leaves blighted—
the gardener a cheat; he left off speaking
and abandoned me.

140

When his mother remembers her lips tremble,
her heart stung to tears.
These birds would not stay in my house.
I could not make them happy,
O Lord!

publ. 1964

The Artist's Visions

Hymn to Apollo

This passage from the beginning of the second canto of *Circe the Enchantress* provides a sample of Devkota's manner of dealing with Greek mythology. The diction of the original Nepali is highly sanskritized, and Vedic names *(Bhāskar, Puruṣa)* are introduced into the Hellenic context.

At daybreak on the morrow
gold seethed in the waters;
soon in the bright sky the disc all gilded
mounted slow.

Then on bended knee, with head bowed down
above the peaceful glimmer of the burnished waves
the heroes sang a hymn of praise to Apollo
God of the Sun.*

"O luminous youth imperishable,
sky-wanderer,
gold-winged ocean bird,
musician of the undying lyre,
eye of the Universe,
Hail!

Live-bodied figure of Mycenean gold,
strike with your rays to bring
yet greater light,
and on this our unknown voyage
protect us, O radiant one!"

Bhāskar, the sun and also an epithet for Shiva.

145

The bright sun smiling,
gold primal male,* diamond-flashing,
blazes in white fire.

A scrap of cloud
alone in the vast azure
like a ship—
cast out of home, without kin, of fallen lineage,
on the lifeline of the waters' weft
without a steersman—
drifted in the blue.
The Grecian heroes watched it
lit to radiance by the sun.

publ. 1967

---

*Puruṣa, in Vedic mythology the original male person and source of the created world.

The Artist

Let people not give, not give!
    I'm content with my world.

Who's calling, who's calling
    in the early morning on the other side?

When you search, when you quest
    why expect food or fodder?

A few days in this jungle, then
    set out for other lands.

The tree grows toward the rose,
    the fountain behind the river.

My heart keeps on singing,
    the beauty before it.

One impulse and one gleam:
    trivial then Kubera* and his wealth.

One lovely flame in the spirit,
    and life like heaven.

The world turned that way, I this—
    both of us mad.

The world picks hard pieces,
    I moonlit clouds.

They say I fly off in the wind,
    my spirit shadow, moonlight my drink.

My life is trying to sing
    like the murmur of forest streams.

publ. 1958

* The god of wealth.

147

Crazy

1.
Oh yes, friend! I'm crazy—
that's just the way I am.

2.
I see sounds,
I hear sights,
I taste smells,
I touch not heaven but things from the underworld,
things people do not believe exist,
whose shapes the world does not suspect.
Stones I see as flowers
lying water-smoothed by the water's edge,
rocks of tender forms
· in the moonlight
when the heavenly sorceress smiles at me,
putting out leaves, softening, glistening,
throbbing, they rise up like mute maniacs,
like flowers, a kind of moon-bird's flowers.
I talk to them the way they talk to me,
a language, friend,
that can't be written or printed or spoken,
can't be understood, can't be heard.
Their language comes in ripples to the moonlit Ganges banks,
ripple by ripple—
oh yes, friend! I'm crazy—
that's just the way I am.

3.
You're clever, quick with words,
your exact equations are right forever and ever.

But in my arithmetic, take one from one—
and there's still one left.
You get along with five senses,
I with a sixth.
You have a brain, friend,
I have a heart.
A rose is just a rose to you—
to me it's Helen and Padmini.
You are forceful prose,
I liquid verse.
When you freeze I melt,
when you're clear I get muddled
and then it works the other way around.
Your world is solid,
mine vapor,
yours coarse, mine subtle.
You think a stone reality;
harsh cruelty is real for you.
I try to catch a dream,
the way you grasp the rounded truth of cold, sweet coin.
I have the sharpness of the thorn,
you of gold and diamonds.
You think the hills are mute—
I call them eloquent.
Oh yes, friend!
I'm free in my inebriation—
that's just the way I am.

    4.
In the cold of the month of Magh
I sat
warming to the first white heat of the star.
The world called me drifty.
When they saw me staring blankly for seven days
after I came back from the burning ghats
they said I was a spook.

149

When I saw the first marks of the snows of time
in a beautiful woman's hair
I wept for three days.
When the Buddha touched my soul
they said I was raving.
They called me a lunatic because I danced
when I heard the first spring cuckoo.
One dead-quiet moon night
breathless I leapt to my feet,
filled with the pain of destruction.
On that occasion the fools
put me in the stocks.
One day I sang with the storm—
the wise men
sent me off to Ranchi.*
Realizing that same day I myself would die
I stretched out on my bed.
A friend came along and pinched me hard
and said, Hey, madman,
your flesh isn't dead yet!
For years these things went on.
I'm crazy, friend—
that's just the way I am.

5.

I called the Navab's wine blood,
the painted whore a corpse,
and the king a pauper.
I attacked Alexander with insults,
and denounced the so-called great souls.
The lowly I have raised on the bridge of praise
to the seventh heaven.
Your learned pandit is my great fool,

* Celebrated madhouse in India, where Devkota spent a few months.

150

your heaven my hell,
your gold my iron,
friend! your piety my sin.
Where you see yourself as brilliant
I find you a dolt.
Your rise, friend—my decline.
That's the way our values are mixed up,
friend!
Your whole world is a hair to me.
Oh yes, friend, I'm moonstruck through and through—
moonstruck!
That's just the way I am.

    6.

I see the blind man as the people's guide,
the ascetic in his cave a deserter;
those who act in the theater of lies
I see as dark buffoons.
Those who fail I find successful,
and progress only backsliding.
Am I squint-eyed,
or just crazy?
Friend, I'm crazy.

Look at the withered tongues of shameless leaders,
the dance of the whores
at breaking the backbone of the people's rights.
When the sparrow-headed newsprint spreads its black lies
in a web of falsehood
to challenge Reason—the hero in myself—
my cheeks turn red, friend,
red as molten coal.
When simple people drink dark poison with their ears
thinking it nectar—
and right before my eyes, friend!—

then every hair on my body stands up stiff
as the Gorgon's serpent hair—
every hair on me maddened!
When I see the tiger daring to eat the deer, friend,
or the big fish the little,
then into my rotten bones there comes
the terrible strength of the soul of Dadhichi*
and tries to speak, friend,
like the stormy day crashing down from heaven with the
   lightning.
When man regards a man
as not a man, friend,
then my teeth grind together, all thirty-two,
top and bottom jaws,
like the teeth of Bhimasena.†
And then
red with rage my eyeballs roll
round and round, with one sweep
like a lashing flame
taking in this inhuman human world.
My organs leap out of their frames—
uproar! uproar!
my breathing becomes a storm,
my face distorted, my brain on fire, friend!
with a fire like those that burn beneath the sea,
like the fire that devours the forests,
frenzied, friend!
as one who would swallow the wide world raw.
Oh yes, my friend,
the beautiful chakora‡ am I,

---

* The legend is that Indra slew the demons with the bones of the sage Dadhi-
chi.
†The strongest of the five Pandava brothers in the *Mahābhārata*.
‡A fabulous bird said to subsist on moonbeams (or, in some legends, fire).

destroyer of the ugly,
both tender and cruel,
the bird that steals the heaven's fire,
child of the tempest,
spew of the insane volcano,
terror incarnate.
Oh yes, friend,
my brain is whirling, whirling—
that's just the way I am.

Publ. 1953

Worn-out Mat

This curious poem is an example of Devkota's sometimes obscure whimsicality. Except for the exclamation marks reproduced here, the original poem is devoid of punctuation.

The way of the mat is
not to try to feed the world

I am the hide of some sun-worshipping sadhu
twisted and hung out
for everybody's dirty feet

this is also one life for me
after death
a net of pain
the outcry
of a sage vowed to silence

this is the final stage
of rivers of nectar!
to be poison also is a personality
the drunkenness of renunciation
is weeping and rotting with worms

my breast today is holes, oh!
today there's come into my bosom
a coiled serpent
a pox on my theories!
the way of the mat is
not to try to feed the world!

publ. 1964

154

Love

Praised more than can be told
in the swaying pleasure groves:
only the eye is pleasured—
by seeing just a little,
the other catches the whole heart,
and the other
seeing one as another (and being lonely)
calls out.

Though new it seems familiar—
did this heart invite it?
The world changed, and perhaps
painfully awakened this forgotten life.
Shiva, perhaps,
to adorn Uma,*
with one glance
dreamed this earth to be their home.

The world must turn to a drop
and disappear
in overflowing eyes.
Every moment every drop of water
must be a creation,
like constellations amid the void.
Somebody weeps
all night, all night,
and creates a heaven.
Divine dream!
This crowd of lonely stars!
Praise be to the life of love.

publ. 1964

*Spouse of Shiva.

155

The Magpie Madly Talking

On that branch of the walnut tree
while roosters steal bits of grain
and dawn stoops to sweep the night away,
in the half-light, best moment of the day,
with a sound clear as bullets,
sharp, sweet—how can I describe it, friend?—
the magpie madly talking.

When the speech swings and sways
a world opens that could not be opened—
the shores of dream and waking.
I find the one who slept with me
has fled—beloved, youthful, shy,
my drunken companion too, suddenly alert,
the one called sleep, rhythm of the night!
the magpie madly talking.

Strange some moments are,
awake smiling, asleep in tears.
How the honey melted in that moment—
the bodhisattva awakened speech.
In that sound the rays cried out,
scaring away night's little Nirvana,
piercing this kind of eternal sleep.
The hinges of the heavenly portals grated,
frightening all the armies of hell,
and the victorious sun climbed up the peaks—
the magpie madly talking.

The dawn goddess swings her broom,
dispersing every shred and tatter,

the dirty garments of snowy palaces.
Tender rays have washed them,
fusing all the colors,
the boiling cauldron suspended,
drenching the sunrise peaks with magic—
the magpie madly talking.

A blossom bent her limbs,
and quickly arranged her raiment
when she heard the speech of the golden age.
Within the chalice of her heart
a pure drop lingered
like a priceless pearl.

That sound struck, piercing me
as I slept, friend,
on the pillow of deepest sleep.
I awakened from a dream—
and how much lovelier the waking light!
snowy white with the first beams;
the golden temple spires
cast their nets to catch fish.
The souls of old Messiahs
awakened and proclaimed,
"Lo, just this brings out the faith!"
And then were heard the whinnying steeds
of the chariot of progress on the sunrise peaks,
tossing their manes.
I cast forth the net of sight
and saw an awakened world.

Revivified the atmosphere!
bright with the blood of martyrs.
Caroling in its voice it said,
"To say 'life' is this, is this—
to laugh and play life's blood-red festival!"

The voice of the age beat against the skies
setting a host of wings in flight
when the magpie began to talk.

All over heaven the tears vanished,
the sky dazzled like a poet's heart.
In a little moment like eternity
I drank the gold flame into my eyes,
victorious the poet sun.
The dawn goddess chose her groom,
chose me—"O dispeller of the dark!
Yours, yours the dawn girl, in your keeping!"
rang out in the mad bird's talk.

Friend, look at the crazy eyes!
Strange brilliance they've caught today.
Song of the rays melting in the ear,
bodiless I blaze, transparent,
like a poet without colors sounding out the age.
My heart is singing life's blood festival.
Fear me, and draw away;
now the naked body turns to fire,
I speak the spark,
I watch the flames—
what's happened to me today?
The earth opens and fragrance issues forth
when the mad bird
in the wet intoxication of its sounds
speaks among the walnut branches.
Today I sing the song of an age to come,
gathering up those sounds,
piercing through deception—
the magpie madly talking!

publ. 1956

158

Last Poem in Nepali

Written on September 4, 1959, ten days before the poet's death. Some of the poem's obscurities come from the total lack of any punctuation in the original, as published by Hari Shresta in a special leaflet, with the title, "From the Deathbed."

> Within this blissful heaven the earth
> I took my pleasure, creating fantasies.
> Like a desert was what it all became.
> As though the night has fallen
> I just now barely understand
> Suddenly the world is like a night.
> So long as I was living I could not grasp it.
> At the end I learned Shri Krishna was the only one,
> but I had no knowledge, no wisdom, and no devotion.
> Hot as an atom in a vast desert
> I burn, dying without hope, dumb.
> I am empty as a dried-out tree,
> heating in the funeral fire I threw off
> my sacraments like water.
> I have lost everything. I disappear
> like emptiness into emptiness.
> In this heaven I was born and thrived;
> at the end, uselessly,
> I turn to ash and disappear.

Devkota on Devkota*

Lekhnath's inspiration (*laharī*) has its origins in Sanskrit. But in Devkota the reflection of English Romantic style is very evident. Many of his poems are filled with exuberant feeling, the worship of beauty, and love of nature. While Lekhnath appears in the guise of a moral teacher giving advice, Devkota, instead of giving advice, is impelled toward an art that touches the heart.

He believes that the nature of true art is to touch the heart, and through the heart to fully involve the intellect. In Balkrishna Sama-ji the poetry comes forth with an effort—the flowers are embroidered with much of the skill of a painter or fine artificer. Devkota's poetry comes flowing forth of itself, without effort . . . the poet like a springtime bird pours out his heart's joy. He does not have to fashion a meter or count syllables or stop often in his writing. In his style are dash, speed, and power. One is often afraid that, like a rivulet, in the rain it may overflow the banks with an excess of power and break the dikes. And one also fears that such a flood, becoming murky, will turn into mud and dirt and tiny bits of gold.

Devkota does not pause to edit, refine or go over a second time, and occasionally the poetry is marked by lack of clarity, confused grammatical structure, and obscurity (*aspaṣṭatā,*

*Translated from "Bhikhārī: Devkoṭā, Śailī ra Bhikhārī Bhāvarth," *Jayantī*, Bhādra 30, v.s. 2027 (September 1970), pp. 1–4, by L. P. Devkota, though written in the third person; date of composition uncertain but probably not long after the publication of the volume *Bhikhārī* (The Beggar) in 1953, though all the poems referred to had been published in journals by 1941.

duranvaya, durbodhatā). He sees the form of the external world as the reflection of his own inner activity.

Or he sees his own profound inner truths shining in the portrayal of nature. For Lekhnath-ji nature is a pleasantly painted canvas or background. But for Laxmiprasad Devkota nature is seen as a living companion or a mine of beauty. In this tendency we find the influence of Wordsworth or Shelley or Keats in him. The flavor of English literature, particularly Romantic literature, makes a profound and colorful impression in this poet who sucks the juice of English literature. In Devkota there is the quality of theism, which takes on a quite different philosophical turn in Lekhnath-ji and is not found at all in Balkrishna Sama-ji. He sees a supreme deity as monarch of the world and the soul as monarch of the body. In a word, his flight has always been toward immortality. In "The Beggar," in the form of the man who comes into the courtyard begging, it is as though a god were standing there, who keeps on calling with the human speech of pain to awaken the soul of man, but this god is not found on the road of blind ritual, the tradition of credulity.

. . . There is no lesson of inactivity in Devkota's dharma. He insists most particularly on service to man: "to the city of the heart I bring a message of service."

Also in Devkota, as in the English poets, particularly Wordsworth, one finds the tendency to idealize childhood. He sees in the child the pure and divine imagination and the life of feeling which it is not possible for man to receive in the grief-shrouded state of adulthood. . . . The portrayal of the greatness of the common man, which is a Romantic quality, is also present in Devkota, as in the description of the greatness of the joyful life in the poem called "The Peasant." Devkota's worship of beauty shines in such poems as "Cāru," "Spring," "Evening," and "The Grasscutter."

He is an enemy of blind tradition, as in "Pilgrim." . . .

The duty of his life he understands to be to make the world shine with the outpouring of inner strength. And similarly, he wishes to persuade others of this duty. Devkota's heart is deeply touched by this feeling of service to man. The holy feeling of the grasscutter lighting a lamp in the heart of the poet Bhanubhakta and illuminating the development of Nepali literature—[Devkota] wishes that there shall be more just such grasscutters and poets filled with the sentiment of divine service to Nepal.

Style:
1. Exuberance and flow.
2. Influence of English Romantic literature.
3. Symbolism—the correspondence of nature and inner truth.
4. Virtue of flow, fault of exaggeration and impetuosity.
5. From *varṇik* verse toward *mātrik* verse.*
6. Affecting the emotions first and through them the intellect.
7. Vividness of the imagination.
8. Not holding to rigid end-rhymes (unlike Lekhnath).
9. Word coinages when necessary.
10. Spring-like luxuriance in the earlier poems, later poems—color ripened with thought.
11. Earlier poems not complicated, mainly simple, despite Sanskrit; in later poems begins the use of too many difficult Sanskrit words.
12. Avoidance of repeating Sanskrit *dhvani* [tone, nuance, allusiveness, resonance]; the *dhvani* is of the new age.

* Both the *varṇik* and *mātrik* metrical systems are quantitative, like the classical meters of Greek and Latin. The *varṇik*, more frequently employed in Sanskrit poetry, consists of strictly ordered patterns of long and short syllables and allows for very little variation. The *mātrik* meters, more popular with poets in the various North Indian vernaculars, permit considerable freedom of patterning, although each new pattern, once established, becomes in its turn a firm and rarely varied basis for the particular poem or stanza. For further details, see A. Berriedale Keith, *A History of Sanskrit Literature* (London: Oxford University Press, 1920; reprinted 1961), pp. 417 ff.; S. H. Kellogg, *A Grammar of the Hindi Language* (London: Routledge & Kegan Paul, 1965), pp. 546 ff.; and Barbara Stoler Miller, *Love Song of the Dark Lord* (New York: Columbia University Press, 1977), pp. 8 ff.

13. Deep inner meanings of words must be brought forth—here and there obscure.
14. Faults of bad syntax, repetitiousness.
15. In diverse feelings and images a unity of central feeling.
16. Emotion dominant over thought.

Sources and Original Titles
of the Poems

Title in Translation	Original Title	Source
Spring	"Vasant"	*Lakśmī Kavitā-Sangrah*
Clearing Morning in the Month of Magh	"Māghko Khuleko Bihāna"	*Cillā Pātharū*
Beans and Rice and Mustard Greens	"Dāl-Bhāt-Ḍuku"	*Indrenī*, no. 3
Unknown	"Avidit"	*Bhāvnā Gāngey*
Cascades	"Jharnā"	*Bhikhārī*
Morning Song	"Prabodh-Gān"	*Chāngāsanga Kurā*
Rainbow	"Indrenī"	*Lakśmī Kavitā-Sangrah*
Minpachas	"Mīnpacās"	*Cillā Pātharū*
To a Dark Cloudy Night	"Saghan Tamisrāprati"	*Indrenī*, no. 7
Dawn	"Prabhāt"	*Ākāś Bolcha*
Pipedreams	"Bhūt Savār"	*Lakśmī Kavitā-Sangrah*
Friday Night Eleven O'Clock	"Śukravār Eghāra Baje Rātī"	*Indrenī*, no. 5
Quatrain	"Ma Lahrā Bhae"	*Lakśmī Kavitā-Sangrah*
The Season of Life	"Zindagīko Mausam"	*Bhikhārī*
Memory	"Samjhanā"	"
Clay Lamp	"Pālā"	*Bhāvnā Gāngey*
Echoes	"Anunād"	*Janmotsav*
The Gaine	"Gāine"	*Gāine Gīt*
To Go On Singing	"Gāūm Gāūm Lāgyo"	"

Title in Translation	Original Title	Source
Foggy Morning	"Kuirī Bihāna"	Gāine Gīt
I Said (1 &2)	"Maile Bhaneṁ"	"
He Said	"Unle Bhane"	"
A Thousand Deaths A Thousand Lives	"Hajār Maraṇ Hajār Jīvan"	"
Sweeper	"Camār"	"
I've Had It	"Bho Hai"	"
Sleeping Coolie	"Nidrit Bhariyā"	Lakśmī Kavitā-Sangrah
The Beggar	"Bhikhārī"	Bhikhārī
Pilgrim	"Yātrī"	"
A Ballad of Rani Pokhri	"Rānīpokhrī"	Bhāvnā Gāngey
Ballad of the Fair Sweeper	"Camār Sundarī"	"
Child of the Times	"Yug Bālak"	Lakśmī Kavitā-Sangrah
Toward Dasain	"Daśaimtāka"	"
Dreams	"Sapnāharū"	Putalī
Remembering	"Samjhanā"	"
Wind Country	"Hāvā Deś"	Ākāś Bolcha
Remembering the Wheat	"Gahūṅko Samjhanā"	Cillā Pātharū
In Memory of Three Deceased Children	"Tīn Svargavāsī Baccāko Samjhanā"	"
Hymn to Apollo	no title	Māyāvinī Sarsī
The Artist	"Kalākār"	Janmotsav
Crazy	"Pāgal"	Indrenī, no. 7
Worn-out Mat	"Saṛeko Sukul"	Cillā Pātharū
Love	"Prem"	"
The Magpie Madly Talking	"Dhobinī Paglī Bolī"	Lakśmī Kavitā-Sangrah
Last Poem in Nepali	no title	Samarpan (privately printed pamphlet)

🔊Bibliography

By Laxmiprasad Devkota

Ākāś Bolcha [The Sky Speaks]. Bhadrapur: Jhapa Prakashan, 1968.
Bhāvnā Gāngey [Thoughts by the Ganges]. Varanasi: Yugvani Prakashan, n.d.
Bhikhārī [The Beggar]. Kathmandu: Sajha Prakashan, 1970.
Bhikhārī, rev. ed. Kathmandu: Sajha Prakashan, 1974.
"Bhikhārī: Devkoṭa, Śailī ra Bhikhārī Bhāvārth" [Beggar: Devkota, Style, and the Substance of "Bhikhārī"], *Jayantī* (Bhadra 30, v.s. 2027; September 1970).
Campā. Kathmandu: Sajha Prakashan, 1972.
Chaharā [Cascades]. Kathmandu: Devkota, 1959.
Chāngāsanga Kurā [Talking with Waterfalls]. Bhadrapur: Jhapa Prakashan, 1969.
Cillā Pātharū [Smooth Leaves]. Kathmandu: Mandevi Devkota, 1966.
Duṣyanta Śakuntalā Bheṭ [The Meeting of Dushyanta and Shakuntala]. Kathmandu: Sajha Prakashan, 1968.
Gāine Gīt [Songs of the Gaine]. Kathmandu: Sajha Prakashan, 1968.
Janmotsav [Birthday]. Kathmandu: Madhusudan Devkota, 1958.
Kaṭak [Army]. Kathmandu: Sajha Prakashan, 1969.
Kṛṣi-Bālā [The Peasant Girl]. Kathmandu: Sajha Prakashan, 1968.
Kunjinī. Kathmandu: Bhaktabahadur, 1966.
Lakśmī Kathā Sangrah [Collection of Devkota Stories]. Kathmandu: Sajha Prakashan, 1975.
Lakśmī Kavitā-Sangrah [Collection of Devkota Poems]. Kathmandu: Sajha Prakashan, 1976.
Lakśmī Nibandha Sangrah [Collection of Devkota Essays]. Kathmandu: Sajha Prakashan, 1961.
Lūnī. Kathmandu: Sajha Prakashan, 1972.
Mahārāṇā Pratāp. Kathmandu: Nepal Samskritik Sangha, 1967.

167

Manoranjan [Entertainments]. Kathmandu: Nepal Samskritik Sangha, 1967.
Māyāvinī Sarsī [Circe the Enchantress]. Varanasi: Nepali Pustak Ghar, 1967.
Mhendu. Kathmandu: Nepali Bhasaprakashini Samiti, 1958.
Munā Madan [Muna and Madan]. Kathmandu: Sajha Prakashan, 1970.
Navras [The Nine Sentiments]. Varanasi: Nepali Sahitya Char, 1968.
Nepālī Śākuntala. Kathmandu: Sajha Prakashan, 1968.
Pramithas [Prometheus]. Kathmandu: Nepal Rajkiy Prajna-Pratisthan, 1975.
Putalī [Butterfly]. Kathmandu: Sajha Prakashan, 1971.
Rājkumār Prabhākar [Prince Prabhakar]. Kathmandu: Sajha Prakashan, 1967.
Rāvaṇ-Jaṭāyu-Yuddha [The Battle of Ravana and Jatayu]. Kathmandu: Nepali Bhasaprakashini Samiti, 1958.
Sāvitrī-Satyavān [Savitri and Satyavan]. Kathmandu: Sajha Prakashan, 1967.
Sītā-Haraṇ [The Abduction of Sita]. Kathmandu: Sajha Prakashan, 1967.
Sulocanā. Kathmandu: Sajha Prakashan, n.d.
Sunko Bihāna [Golden Morning]. Kathmandu: Sajha Prakashan, 1971.
Van Kusum. Kathmandu: Sajha Prakashan, 1968.

General Reference, Anthologies, and Journals

Acharya, Jaya Raj. "Nepalese Poetry After Devkota: A Brief Survey," *The Rising Nepal,* 7 October 1977.
Bandhu. *Mahākavi Lakśmī Prasād Devkoṭā.* Kathmandu: Bhanu Prakashan, 1969.
Baral, Ishwar. "Balkrishna Sama," *Kailash* (1974), vol. 2, no. 3.
Bhānu (Devkoṭā Viśeṣānk) [Special Devkota Issue] (v.s. 2025 Phagun; February–March 1965), year 5, no. 12.
Clark, T. W. "The Rani Pokhri Inscription, Kathmandu," *Bulletin of the School of Oriental and African Studies* (1957), vol. 20.
Current Trends in Linguistics, vol. 5, *Linguistics in South Asia,* ed. Thomas A. Sebeok. Leiden: Mouton, 1969.
Indrenī (1956), vols. 1–7.

Joshi, Kumarbahadur. *Mahākavi Devkoṭā ra Unkā Mahākāvya* [Devkota and His Narrative Poetry]. Kathmandu: Sahyogi Prakashan, 1974.

Kavitā (Winter 1965), year 2, no. 1.

Keith, A. Berriedale. *A History of Sanskrit Literature.* London: Oxford University Press, 1920; rpt. 1961.

Kellogg, S. H. *A Grammar of the Hindi Language.* Rpt., London: Routledge & Kegan Paul, 1965.

Kurve, Marvin. "Napal [sic] Writers Discuss Problems," *The Times of India,* 6 October 1972.

Miller, Barbara Stoler. *Love Song of the Dark Lord.* New York: Columbia University Press, 1977.

Modern Nepali Poems. Kathmandu: Royal Nepal Academy, 1972.

Monier-Williams, M., et al. *A Sanskrit-English Dictionary.* Rpt., Delhi: Motilal Banarsidass, 1970.

Moraes, Dom. *Gone Away.* Boston: Little, Brown, 1960.

Nav Padya-Sangrah [New Anthology of Poetry]. Kathmandu: Bhaktabahadur Publishers & Booksellers, 1953.

Nepālī Padyasangrah [Anthology of Nepali Poetry]. 2 vols. Kathmandu: Sajha Prakashan, 1970.

Pande, Nityaraj. *Mahākavi Devkoṭā.* Lalitpur: Madan Puruskar Guthi, 1960.

Pandey, Mathuradatta. *Nepālī aur Hindī ke Bhaktikāvya kā Tulnātmak Adhyayan* [Comparative Study of Nepali and Hindi Devotional Poetry]. Delhi: Bharatiy Grantha Niketan, 1970.

Pant, Mahes Raj, and Aishvarya Dhar Sharma. *The Two Earliest Copper-plate Inscriptions from Nepal. Kathmandu: Nepal Research Centre, 1977.*

Pokharel, Balkrishna. *Nepālī Bhāṣā ra Sāhitya* [Nepali Language and Literature]. Kathmandu: Ratna Pustak Bhandar, 1964.

Pradhan, Parasmani. *Pāṅc Paurakhī Puruṣratna* [Five Great Heroes]. Kalimpong: Bhagyalakshmi Prakashan, 1969.

Racanā (Lakśmiprasād Devkoṭā-Ank) [Devkota Memorial Issue] (v.s. 2033, Pus-Magh; December-February, 1976–1977), year 14, no. 4.

Risal, Rammani. *Nepālī Kāvya ra Kavi* [Nepali Poetry and Poets]. Kathmandu: Sajha Prakashan, 1974.

Sājhā Kavitā. Kathmandu: Sajha Prakashan, 1967.

Sājhā Samālocanā. Kathmandu: Sajha Prakashan, 1968.

Satyal, Yajnaraj. *Nepālī Sāhityako Bhūmikā* [Introduction to Nepali Literature]. Kathmandu: Ratna Pustak Bhandar, 1969.

Sharma, Bal Chandra. *Nepālī Śabda-Koś* [Nepali Dictionary]. Kathmandu: Royal Nepal Academy, 1962.

Sharma, Janaklal. *Mahākavi Devkoṭā: Ek Vyaktitva, Duī Racanā* [Devkota: One Personality, Two Creations]. Kathmandu: Sajha Prakashan, 1975.

Sharma, Sharadchandra. *"Bhikhārī"-Sahāyak* [Guide to "Bhikhārī"]. Kathmandu: Ratna Pustak Bhandar, 1970.

Shrestha, Hari. *Devkoṭā Samjhera* [Remembering Devkota]. Kathmandu: Ramesh Shrestha, 1965.

Tanasarma. *Nepālī Sāhityako Itihās* [History of Nepali Literature]. Kathmandu: Sahyogi Prakashan, 1970.

Tripathi, Vasudev. *Siṁhāvlokan*. [A Review of the Past]. Kathmandu: sajha Prakashan, 1970.

Turner, Ralph Lilley. *A Comparative and Etymological Dictionary of the Nepali Language*. London: Routledge & Kegan Paul, 1931.

Van Buitenen, J. A. *The Mahabharata*. Vol. 2, *The Book of the Assembly Hall*. Chicago: University of Chicago Press, 1976.

Modern Asian Literature Series

Neo-Confucian Studies

Translations from the Oriental Classics

The Romance of the Western Chamber (Hsi Hsiang chi), tr.
S. I. Hsiung. Also in paperback ed.   1968
The Manyōshū, Nippon Gakujutsu Shinkōkai edition.
Paperback text edition.   1969
Records of the Historian: Chapters from the Shih chi of Ssu-
ma Ch'ien. Paperback test edition, tr. Burton Wat-
son   1969
Cold Mountain: 100 Poems by the T'ang Poet Han-shan, tr.
Burton Watson. Also in paperback ed.   1970
Twenty Plays of the Nō Theatre, ed. Donald Keene. Also
in paperback ed.   1970
Chūshingura: The Treasury of Loyal Retainers, tr. Donald
Keene. Also in paperback ed.   1971
The Zen Master Hakuin: Selected writings, tr. Philip B.
Yampolsky   1971
Chinese Rhyme-Prose: Poems in the Fu Form from the Han
and Six Dynasties Periods, tr. Burton Watson. Also in
paperback ed.   1971
Kūkai: Major Works, tr. Yoshito S. Hakeda   1972
The Old Man Who Does as He Pleases: Selections from the
Poetry and Prose of Lu Yu, tr. Burton Watson   1973
The Lion's Roar of Queen Śrīmālā, tr. Alex and Hideko
Wayman   1974
Courtier and Commoner in Ancient China: Selections from
the History of The Former Han by Pan Ku, tr. Burton
Watson. Also in paperback ed.   1974
Japanese Literature in Chinese. Vol. I: Poetry and Prose in
Chinese by Japanese Writers of the Early Period, tr.
Burton Watson   1975
Japanese Literature in Chinese. Vol. II: Poetry and Prose in
Chinese by Japanese Writers of the Later Period, tr.
Burton Watson   1976
Scripture of the Lotus Blossom of the Fine Dharma, tr.
Leon Hurvitz. Also in paperback ed.   1976
Love Song of the Dark Lord: Jayadeva's Gītagovinda, tr.

Barbara Stoler Miller. Also in paperback ed. Cloth
ed. includes critical text of the Sanskrit. 1977
Ryōkan: Zen Monk-Poet of Japan, tr. Burton Watson 1977
*Calming the Mind and Discerning the Real: From the Lam
rim chen mo of Tsoṅ-kha-pa,* tr. Alex Wayman 1978
*The Hermit and the Love-Thief: Sanskrit Poems of Bhar-
trihari and Bilhaṇa,* tr. Barbara Stoler Miller 1978

Studies in Oriental Culture

Companions to Asian Studies

A Guide to Oriental Classics, ed. Wm. Theodore de Bary
and Ainslie T. Embree, 2d ed. Also in paperback
ed.   1975

Introduction to Oriental Civilizations
Wm. Theodore de Bary, *Editor*

Sources of Japanese Tradition 1958 Paperback ed., 2 vols. 1964
Sources of Indian Tradition 1958 Paperback ed., 2 vols. 1964
Sources of Chinese Tradition 1960 Paperback ed., 2 vols. 1964